SILENT
AND
GRATEFUL TEARS

SILENT
AND
GRATEFUL TEARS

LIZ TOBIN FALZONE

Copyright © 2012 by Liz Tobin Falzone.

Library of Congress Control Number:		2012919359
ISBN:	Hardcover	978-1-4797-3422-1
	Softcover	978-1-4797-3421-4
	Ebook	978-1-4797-3423-8

All rights reserved. No part of this book may be reproduced or transmitted in any form or by any means, electronic or mechanical, including photocopying, recording, or by any information storage and retrieval system, without permission in writing from the copyright owner.

This book was printed in the United States of America.

To order additional copies of this book, contact:
Xlibris Corporation
1-888-795-4274
www.Xlibris.com
Orders@Xlibris.com

Contents

Chapter 1.   Burning Memories 13
Chapter 2.   Dark Days of Pain 22
Chapter 3.   The Sergeant at Arms 28
Chapter 4.   Angels in Black and White 31
Chapter 5.   The Unexplained 35
Chapter 6.   The Door Opens 39
Chapter 7.   The Voice 42
Chapter 8.   The Looking Glass 47
Chapter 9.   Modeling 53
Chapter 10. The Business 66
Chapter 11. The Unexpected 80
Chapter 12. Hollywood 92
Chapter 13. War of the Worlds 99
Chapter 14. Stepmom—Limo 105
Chapter 15. The Cancer 111
Chapter 16. The Music 116
Chapter 17. God, Please Not Again 121
Chapter 18. A Little Bit of Heaven 124
Chapter 19. Rubber duckies lead way to fun at
             annual festival in Beacon Falls 130
Chapter 20. New Pals 136
Chapter 21. Flowers to Roar About 137
Chapter 22. Forgiveness Why Not! 138

Dedication

Silent and
Grateful

Tears

Liz Tobin Falzone

I dedicate this book
to my loving father,
who saved my life.

To God who gave me
strength to survive.

To my husband
who taught me to live,
laugh, and forgive.

To my daughter
who gave me
the opportunity to
become a loving
and caring mother.

And
to my mother
who unknowingly
made me stronger.

When you are born, you are given your birth date.
When you pass on, you are given that date on your headstone.
These dates are there, but what really counts is the time between these dates.
The dash—is what really counts.
What you have achieved and what you have done to improve the life of another.

Preface

I have written this book to share with you, the reader, how it is possible to achieve your dreams. If you have experienced abuse or bullying by your peers or family members, it is possible to open doors that have securely been locked shut by others not wanting people to know the truths that lie beneath to be known.

I have known a place where no one is there to understand your pain. A place where you try to escape the neglect by making a world of make-believe, a world of kings and queens, trying to enjoy all those things that children have a given birthright to enjoy.

I will share with you how I turned the negative in my life to positive achievements. Travel with me through my young adult life. Starting my own business and working with major movie stars. Having the opportunity to change the lives of people that led me to create a music CD for cancer survivors. How I managed to finish college and earn my degree.

I accomplished more than I ever thought possible. I found faith, strength, love, and forgiveness. Remember that no matter what life throws at us, we all have the courage to change the outcome. You can make a difference in a small or big way. What really matters is that you tried. You can do it! You can even change a person's life for the better, and helping each other to bring comfort and hope is what life is really all about, isn't it?

Introduction

The story starts out in the fifties in Bridgeport, Connecticut. Where low—to middle-class people could earn a living by working as a laborer in one of the many factories usually located in the poorest neighborhoods.

The story is an uplifting journey of a little girl who falls between the cracks and manages to beat the odds. She grew up not only changing her life but the lives of others.

She escapes from the mental and physical abuse and creates a life full of exciting adventures, finds love, and makes the impossible come true.

Bridgeport, the place where she lived, was kind of a melting pot for various ethnic backgrounds. The street she lived on was very common to most streets in the east side of Bridgeport.

A corner market was the focal point for shopping. Ice cream trucks would travel the local streets every night to sell to the residents and their families. The liquor store was where some people would go to buy their beer or wine and escape the reality of their lives. The local junk man would travel the neighborhood with his wagon, selling all kinds of things and sometimes buying items from the local people.

This story tells about two people who came from different backgrounds in Ireland and met here in the United States and became husband and wife and the resentment of the woman who wanted more from life than she got and how this resentment was placed upon the child she did not want.

Burning Memories

Here I am. Who would have thought I would live a life like I have, working with movie stars and having my own talent management. I have had the opportunity to work with famous directors and actors like Steven Spielberg, Barry Levinson, and Brian De Palma, and actors like Julia Roberts, Whoopi Goldberg, and Bette Midler. These are but a few.

I can still see in my mind the six-family tenement house where it all started out and where I spent most of my childhood. It was like a long trailer, one room after another, almost like those long things called buses. The house was in a cluster of other six-family houses.

Across the street was a corner store that sold cold cuts and a lot of canned foods. The yard, if you wanted to call it that, was a driveway that was used for the few who had cars. There were six garages that had big gray doors in front of them. On the side of one of the houses was an outside cellar door hatchway that was the focal point of play because it was sort of a cove located where the garbage cans were kept, and it was considered a safe place to play.

When it came time to take a bath, we had a steel tub that had to be pulled out of the closet because the bathroom was small and had no bathtub or sink. The tub had to be filled with hot water from the sink, and then the cold water was added. There was no privacy because the tub was brought into the kitchen, so you had to take the bath usually late at night. You ended up taking a bath maybe twice a week, and in between time, you would just use a washcloth for your face and whatever you could do with some sense of privacy.

In the bedroom, there were these things in the wall, which I later found out were gaslights. I guess we didn't need them; we did have electricity after all. The stove in the kitchen had a canister in the back of it for fuel, and that was how the house was heated.

The house had a common hallway. The front of the building had a porch on each level that belonged to the family who lived on that floor. The view from the porch was the street and the six-family houses on the other side of the street.

It was a depressing area. I remember one time, a family was put out of their apartment with all their furniture, and the kids were sitting on their couch crying. They could not pay the rent and were put out on the street. I remember always wondering if the same thing could happen to us.

Then there was the woman who threw herself off the second-floor porch. I remember seeing her slipper lying on the pavement. I thought, *Why would she do that?* I knew she didn't have any children and maybe she felt alone, but I couldn't understand what could have led to her committing suicide. The neighbors stood there watching the ambulance take her away. Her dog would cry every night for her. He would climb on the banister of the porch and would lie there, howling. I could hear him at night when I was in bed, and I would start to cry for him and feel how lonely he was. After a week or so, he stopped. To this day, I can't bear to hear the cry of any animal.

A little comfort with a dog named Butch

The neighbors talked about what had happened, and I guess no one ever really knew the reason she did what she did, but the husband and the dog moved away shortly after that.

My good times were when I went with my father for walks on the Boston Green not too far from the house. It was a stretch of grass and trees in the middle of a roadway.

My Dad with my Mother when she was eight months pregnant with me

We would walk to the end of a street across from the green where there was a slaughterhouse; of course, I didn't know it was that then, but I soon found out what it really was. I used to think it was a place where they kept little pigs and cows, until one day, on a Saturday, we walked in as usual to look at the little pigs, and I heard screams. They had a cow on a hook, and they were hitting it with bats and were putting it in a tub of hot, steaming water, and it was crying out in pain. I ran out in tears, and I never wanted to go back there again as you might guess. I knew, even at six years old, that I was going to get out of this place where there was so much pain everywhere I looked. I wanted better, so I promised myself that I was going to have a better life.

I know, of course, that my dad would have never taken me there if he knew they were slaughtering on that particular Saturday. I guess he felt it was a way of giving me some sense of joy by seeing the cows and the little piglets. He was brought up on a potato farm in Limerick, Ireland. His family was poor, and because of this, he had a side to him that was gentle and loving of God's creatures.

There wasn't much to see around our house, nothing that would give you a sense of joy or appreciation of nature. The only other place was Beardsley Park, a distance from the house that sometimes my dad and I would walk to on a nice day. It would take at least an hour or so to walk with my little legs. I loved my walks with my dad. He was a kind man in my eyes. I always knew I was loved when I was with him.

Everyone in the neighborhood would stop to talk to my dad. In the summertime, the ice cream truck would come up the street, and my dad would meet the truck, and if any of the neighborhood kids were around, he would buy them an ice cream cone. There were many times that my dad would walk away without a cone for himself because he just didn't have any money left for himself.

My memory of my mom was that she always seemed unhappy and wished her life was somewhere else with someone else. It was no secret that she didn't love my father, and she let him know, along with my sister and myself.

She was an attractive woman who always dressed up when going out to a function from work without my father.

She didn't seem to want him around her. I knew he drank every Friday night and would come home late from Doyle's Bar, but I didn't understand why she was so against him going anywhere with her. My father was not even allowed to visit the cousins' house with us.

I was told later in life that she was ashamed of getting pregnant with me by my father. This information I certainly didn't need to hear; after all, isn't your mother supposed to love you no matter what? My aunt said that my mother was afraid of what the neighbors would say about her getting pregnant at such a later time in her life, in her late 30s, which then was considered a no-no. My mother confirmed this by telling me when I was about eleven years old that I was never supposed to be born. She told me I was a mistake. She even went into detail and said that I was conceived in New York. After she had gone to a Yankees baseball game with my father, her sister, and her sister's husband and after a couple of drinks, things happened. I guess a lesson to learn is to be careful of your consumption of liquor!

Every Friday night was the night from hell. My father would get home from the bar around one or two in the morning, and then the yelling and shouting and physical abuse would start. I would try to stop the fights by getting between them both. Sometimes, it would work, and other times, I was yelled at and told to go to bed. I would lie there crying and praying, hoping it would stop. Then finally, it was quiet. My father would go to bed, the bed that my mother never shared with my father, and my mother would sit up in the kitchen with her gallon of red wine, drinking one glass after another, and then she would go to sleep on the couch in the living room.

I didn't realize that the fact that my mother and father not sleeping together in the same bed was not the norm until I was playing with my friend Carol at her house. We went into her mom's bedroom to get some makeup to play with, and I realized that her mom and dad shared the room together. I asked her where her father slept, and she answered without hesitation, "Here with my mom."

I always knew something was wrong with my mother. I remember getting up one night because I couldn't sleep, and she was drinking her bottle of wine that she usually hid in the closet. Her arms were stretched out, holding her palms like she was actually feeling the nails from our Lord's hands when he was crucified. She scared me. Did she have powers or was she just nuts?

Some nights, she would come into my room and wake me up, shaking me. I remember the look on her face; it was filled with hate. After a while, I got so used to her crazy behavior that I would let her shake me, and I never said a word. I just looked up at her, wondering what I had done to deserve such hate. When she was done (I don't remember how long the shaking lasted), I would try to go back to sleep. It was then I realized just how much she wished I had never been born, but I never realized to what extent her hate was.

My mother handled all the money that was brought into the house. She would give my dad a sort of allowance. My mother, on the other hand, always seemed to have enough money to get the things she wanted. Granted we didn't have much, but she always looked nice and well dressed. My mother was not a giving person. I know because there were so many times I wore the same old clothes over and over again. I used to feel ashamed when I saw all the other kids in new dresses and clothes. There was even a time when a neighbor talked to my mom about why I was always in the same clothes and why she couldn't buy me a new dress for a particular birthday party that her little sister was going to. I never knew the outcome of that conversation, but nothing different even happened.

I remember one time when I was going downtown with my father on a Saturday. We stopped in to see my mother where she was working at a clothing store. I had seen a red dress, a nice dress you would wear on a Sunday or going to a birthday party, and I fell in love with it. I asked my dad if *I could* get the dress, and I guess he had seen the look in my eyes. He pulled out his wallet with the small amount of money he had from his allowance from my mother and bought me the dress. Going home, I could sense the fear in my father of how my mother would respond to him buying me the dress, and I guess he was right because the minute my mother saw the dress, the fighting started. I never lived down that dress; my mother always found a way to throw it at me and the fact that my father bought it for me.

My father and myself

Dark Days of Pain

As you know, abuse can be mental or physical. I was the unlucky one who got both.

My sister, who was eleven years older than me and who was the center of attention because of her hearing impairment, didn't want another kid to compete with.

From the very beginning, she was resentful of my presence. It was later that I would realize it wasn't just sibling rivalry. No, it was a lot more!

As I got older, I began to realize the hate she had for me was only magnified by my mother's resentment toward me.

One time, my sister was supposed to help me learn to skate. I was six years old at that time. My father had gotten me a pair of roller skates from somewhere. I was just so happy to have them. I didn't care if they were old. I had seen some kids in the neighborhood skating, and I wanted to be like the rest of the kids. One morning, he asked my sister to help me to learn how to skate after school.

I couldn't quite get staying up on both feet, and I was falling a lot. After a while, I asked my sister to help me up, and she grabbed my arms and dragged me along the block for quite a long time. I remember crying and telling her she was hurting me, but she just kept dragging me. I finally broke her grip, and my knees were bleeding, and the skin was torn off one of my knees.

She took off my skates, and I walked home bleeding. When my mother got home from her part-time job, I didn't even get a chance to tell her what happened. My sister ran over to her and told her I fell off the curb and hurt myself. My mother didn't want to hear anything else, and the way my sister looked at me, I realized she could hurt me again if I said anything different, so I let my mother put some bandages on me and that was that.

One other time, she had some friends over the house listening to music. She told me to go outside, so I did. By this time, I learned to listen to her or else. Well, I had been outside for a long time, and I had to go the bathroom. I knocked on the kitchen door window. She saw me and just kept on talking to her girlfriend, then they went into the other room and left me standing there. I felt I was going to wet my pants, so I knocked on the window harder. She wouldn't come to the door. In desperation, I banged on the window harder, and it broke. My hand went right through the window, and I was badly bleeding with a piece of glass still in my hand. She finally came out of the other room and told me I was crazy. I tried to tell her I had to go to the bathroom, but she didn't want to listen. She just pulled the glass from my hand and gave me a towel to wrap around it, and when it finally stopped bleeding, I put a larger bandage on it. When my mom got home, my sister told her that I slammed the door and my hand went through the glass. I knew it was useless to even explain.

One time, my sister made me kneel by the corner of the stove in the kitchen. Why, I really don't remember. I was there so long that I fainted and fell from the heat or something and banged my head on the back of the stove. I got up as usual and went through the day again.

The one time that I was really lucky was the time she pushed me down the flight of stairs from our second-floor apartment in the six-family house we lived in. I, again, never knew the reason she decided to push me. I guess that she thought it was fun to see me get hurt. The stairs were located outside of the landing of our second-floor apartment. I was falling for what seemed to be forever, and I thought I would die. I was afraid that I would go through the railing and fall to the concrete, but I finally got to the bottom of the stairs. I guess it made such a noise that the woman who lived on the first floor came out to see what had happened. She was scared and concerned for me; I was bleeding from my head. She brought me into her house and bandaged me up. She called my mother at work and told her that my sister pushed me down the stairs and that she saw her standing there just looking down at me. Helen asked her if she should bring me to the hospital, and my mother said no, I would be all right. Helen, a nice little Polish woman, had me stay with her and told me to keep awake, and I remember her walking me around her little apartment. When my mother got home from her part-time job at Levitz Department Store, she insisted that Ann didn't mean to push me; it was an accident. My tears and my trying to tell her it wasn't an accident didn't matter.

The funny part of all this was I loved my sister. I thought, when I was in kindergarten and first grade, how cool it was to have an older sister to be my friend and watch over me. I thought, no matter how bad things got, I wouldn't be alone. I was wrong, and it is wrong to think that anyone of any age has the right to abuse you mentally or physically. No one has the right to make you feel bad or to control you.

I would say to anyone younger or older who felt they were being abused to speak up and know that you are special and a unique individual, and if you feel you are being mistreated, find someone you can trust to talk to. It could be a friend, a teacher, anyone and let them know what's happening.

I guess I was the outcast kid on the block where I lived. Across the street was a nice Italian family with a little girl who was really beautiful with long blond hair, and she always was dressed nice. There was the girl upstairs from me with red hair and the temper to go with it, and the lady downstairs with her daughter, Ann.

I never could figure out why they always had nice clothes and looked so nice; after all, we all lived in the same neighborhood. Our fathers worked in the factories that were in the same neighborhood; they must have made about the same amount of money. The other kids' moms didn't work like my mom; she worked at a clothing store downtown Bridgeport.

One Saturday, I went to the playground in the neighborhood, and when I went downstairs in the church to go to the bathroom, I saw a little girl with her foot in the sink, washing off the dirt from the playground. I thought it was kind of strange, so I asked her what she was doing. She said that if she went home dirty that her mother wouldn't like that. We started talking, and she told me to come home with her. I was so lonely for a friend, someone to talk to, I said yes. I walked home with her, and when we got to the top of the stairs, her older sister was upset with her for being late and told me to go home. I was really sad, but I walked back home.

One day, a group of kids were playing in the back of the house, and the redhead from upstairs started calling me names. Little did I know that the woman who lived next door was visited by her mother and her little sister who was the same little girl I had met at the playground. Her mother heard the name-calling and told Alyce to go over and play with me. That was the start of our friendship, which has lasted a lifetime.

SCHOOL DAYS 56-57

Alyce my best and longest friend.
The little girl I met in the playground.
From 1956 to present 2012

The Sergeant at Arms

Aunt May, let's not forget her. She was a strict-looking woman. She always wore her fox fur around her neck and always had a hat, some with veils in noticeable colors, like red or purple. She was tall and lean, and she knew it. The dresses she wore were always straight and belted. She was sort of attractive in a way, like an old-time movie star. Her face was always stern-looking; I don't remember her having much of a smile.

My aunt took my mother in when she came over from Ireland. My mother's father had been a kind of a big shot in their town of Tipperary in Ireland, but he lost everything because of his drinking and then lost his position. I was told he was the first in town to have a company car that he drove around town in.

My mother lived with Aunt May, from what I was told, for a very long time, and my aunt, who was a nurse, got her enrolled in a program at that time to become a kind of baby nurse or nanny. I found out later that my mother wasn't very good at that position; who would have guessed!

My aunt lived in a more upscale section of Bridgeport. Back in those days, the North End was a place of huge homes where doctors and lawyers lived. The house had large lamps with shades that had fringes on them, huge mirrors with gold frames, and crystal lights in the dining room, a far cry from my house.

I used to be sent over to her house at least once a month for the weekend. I always wondered why I was sent there. She had one son, who was never home. He was somewhat older than me, so most of the time was spent with her because Uncle Dave was working. Every time I went over there, I felt that I was not quite good enough. She always checked me over like I was a dog and always insisted on me taking a bath as soon as I got into the house. The baths were always in very hot water. I was used to shutting my mouth when I was feeling bad, so that is exactly what I did.

Until one day, I came over, put my things in the guest bedroom, and then it was bath time. I remember the water being hotter than ever, and as I got into the tub, I let out a scream. The water actually burned my leg. I told her it was too hot; she pushed me into the bathtub and said that I was a big baby, and then she took out a brush. As I was crying and trying to get out of the tub, she pushed me down into the hot water and started scrubbing my back and my arms. When I finally got out of the water, my skin was red and burning. I went to bed again asking, *Why, why me?*

One might ask where my uncle was. When things happened, why didn't he say something to my aunt? I don't know the exact answer to that question, but I do know that in some cases, unfortunately, the other person in the household is in denial or afraid of the repercussions that they might face for acknowledging the situation.

Angels in Black and White

Catholic schools back in those days were strict; even looking the wrong way at the wrong time was looked upon badly. The nuns, for the most part, were very strict.

I remembered one day I couldn't keep the rule about being in the playground at least ten minutes before the doors were let open and we were allowed in the classroom. One morning I was late getting to school. I had to go to the grocery store and buy my lunch, as usual, on Friday morning, but this Friday was different. My mother had her late night on Thursday, drinking herself to sleep as usual, but often, she would not make my lunch and just leave a couple of dollars on the table. This meant to go to the grocery store and get my own lunch, usually a cheese or salami sandwich. This Friday, there were more people in the store, and Bernie, the owner, was talking to one of the men from the street. I kept on trying to get his attention, but he just kept on talking. I knew I was running late, but I didn't want to go to school without my lunch, and I didn't want the other kids to know that my mom didn't care enough to fix my lunch. After all, I was only seven years old. I finally got to the school ground, running all the way. I saw the kids in line, going into the door. One of the nuns, who was very strict, saw me, closed the door, and through the window said, "You stay right there and wait for me to let you in, you know the rules!" It was winter and cold. I stood there, afraid to move until she finally opened the door after what seemed to be at least a half hour or more. I am not really sure of the exact time, but my face burned from the cold.

The light in the storm was a sweet nun named Sister Borgiere. I remember her asking me if I would like to help her clean the upper church of Saint Charles and the convent chapel on Fridays after school. I was so happy to help her; I really liked her, and the other kids thought that was just the greatest thing. I remember the first Friday when I started to help her clean. She took me on a little tour of the convent. She showed me the kitchen, and I saw one of the nuns making the sign of the cross over the loaf of bread that she was cutting.

She also showed me her room. It had another name, but I don't remember what it was; I think it was called a chamber. I noticed that the room was small. She had a bed and a nightstand with some drawers and an area where she hung her robes. I asked her why she didn't have any mirrors in her room, and she said, "Elizabeth, that is because I took a vow to only work for God, that I am his servant and should have no false pride or be concerned with my looks." It was amazing to me how she always looked so beautiful.

One day, while I was working in the chapel of the convent, I started singing as I was scrubbing the stairs of the altar. I heard a voice call out to me, a voice that said, "Elizabeth, I am with you." I looked up at the altar, and I saw a kind of cloud with the face of Jesus, and I knew from that day on that God and Mary would always be there for me.

I told Sister Borgiere about what I saw, and she said to pray to Mary that she would be my mother and help me always. To this day, I always pray to her, and she has never let me down.

One day, Sister Borgiere heard me singing while I was cleaning the altar and said, "Elizabeth, you have a beautiful voice." She decided to have me sing to all the classes on special holidays. Some of the small kids made fun of me, but I didn't care.

Now I knew, no matter what, I had a *voice*!

Angels in Black and White
Sister Borgiere

The Unexplained

I remember one time, my best friend Alyce and I were in the basement of her sister's house. We were decorating for a birthday party for Alyce. We were only thirty days apart with our birthdays, and this was going to be her big ten-year-old party.

Alyce's father was in the hospital. I don't remember what he was in for, but I didn't think it was very serious, or we wouldn't be planning a birthday party. I was standing on a chair putting up some paper decorations, and for no reason at all, I felt this feeling of sorrow; I didn't know why. I knew Mr. Labare and all of Alyce's family. They were nice people, and I used to go over to the house to play with Alyce. I looked down at Alyce, and the words just flowed from my mouth. I said, "Your father just died." Alyce looked at me, and just as she started yelling at me, the phone rang. In a short time, we could hear Joyce, her sister, screaming and crying. It was the hospital; her father just passed away.

The experiences didn't stop. They continued through my life in different ways. I would have dreams, and the dream would come to life.

One time, I was dreaming that I was wearing something yellow, and there was blood on some yellow material. In a couple of days, I accidentally put my hand through the glass pane of the french door in my apartment. I had gotten up during the night for a glass of water, and when the door swung back at me, my hand went through one of the panes of glass. I happened to be wearing a yellow nightgown, which I didn't wear too much because I really didn't like it, but my other nightgowns were in the laundry. I realized, after the bleeding stopped, that the dream had come true.

While visiting a friend and her husband in Vermont, I had a dream of a fire one night where the people were speaking a language I didn't understand, and I heard people screaming and saw them running away from a multifamily house. And there was fire all around the building. The next day, I had slept in late, and my friend knocked on the door to wake me up. She was concerned; she asked if I was ok. I told her of what I had dreamt and how frightening it was to me. When they got their newspaper later that day, they both were surprised to see that there was a fire in another part of the town where a multifamily apartment house with some Spanish-speaking people had caught on fire.

One time I was waiting in the emergency room with my sister. Her boyfriend had a heart attack, and we were waiting to hear how he was doing. In the waiting room was a woman sitting with a small boy. I kept on looking at her, and then I looked her in the eyes and told her that her son was coming out of surgery, and he was going to be fine. She stared at me. How did I know that she had a son in surgery? No one said anything about her son. No doctor, no nurse, no one. Within seconds, a doctor came out, sat next to her, and said her son came out of surgery just fine. The doctor left, and before she left to see her son, she came over to me, placed her hand on mine, and said, "Thank you, God bless!"

I always wondered why I had these experiences. Did I channel some intense avenue of thought, something beyond the natural? Was it because of my fearful childhood, or was it that God gave me this insight to deal with the world and to help those who felt fear of their own?

I always knew that these experiences would not be called normal in today's world. I ask myself, *What is truly normal?* We all know that there are lines to draw in our society; that is how professionals can determine who is safe and should be allowed in our society, but we must admit that when it comes to spiritual experiences, there are things we just don't have an explanation for. Doctors are more and more believing that there is something that can't be explained when their patients recover from terminal conditions after prayer. Many medical professionals can't explain the things that patients see or experience while under anesthesia or in a coma or even when the time is near, like in hospice care.

These experiences would last with me throughout my life, and I pray that I use these gifts as God saw fit. I have always had a true love of God and a devotion to his mother, Mary. I even had the opportunity to direct the first living station of the cross for my church. The experience was something I will never forget. In the first production, my husband, Sal, played Jesus as we created the effect of lightning and thunder during the crucifixion of Jesus, with the lights inside of the church flickering on and off and the soundtrack of thunder. A beautiful stained glass window in the church was located behind the altar. Suddenly, as Sal recited his lines, "FORGIVE THEM, FATHER. THEY KNOW NOT WHAT THEY DO," the sky grew dark outside, and the lightning poured through the stained window. Everyone in church was just shocked and in awe of what had just happened and how the lightning came out of nowhere.

The Door Opens

After graduation from Saint Charles Grammar School, I decided to go to Harding High School, or should I say I didn't have a choice. My mom was not about to pay for a Catholic high school, and I guess I was kind of happy about that. I wanted some freedom!

High school was a whole new experience for me; I was on my own. I could make my own choices about subjects and school activities. I volunteered for the school's newspaper. I auditioned for the singing group, the Madrigals, which was considered a pretty great group to belong to. I also signed up for the drama club, and I made some good friends.

Because of my grades, I was one of the first students to be asked if I would like to work for credits in Bridgeport Hospital and get paid at the same time; of course, I said yes.

The job in Bridgeport Hospital was a good experience for me. I learned a lot about nutrition. I worked in the diet kitchen with the head dietician. She put me in charge of the nutritional shakes; the shakes were for patients who had problems chewing or had stomach problems.

I worked there for about a year and a half. I gained the trust of the dietician, and she asked if I would like to go up on the floors to help patients with their diet choices and then report back to her. Talking with the patients was something I loved. The whole experience gave me a sense of worth, doing something for someone else.

Little did I know that I would be using the lessons I learned with the dietician later in my business, especially since I came across cases of anorexia with some of the models and was able to recognize the symptoms of the disease.

The idea of having some of my own money to buy some new clothes was something I couldn't pass up. My mom didn't buy me many outfits, and so I used to wear the same clothes over and over again, trying to change the look as much as I could. It was difficult to watch other kids in school having different outfits for every day. I had to pay my mom some money from my check that I earned, working at the hospital in the diet kitchen. She called it board, but with whatever I had left, I went to the discount store and bought whatever I could that I thought I could make something out of. I guess I acquired a flair for fashion, making something out of nothing, and it worked. I guess because some boys in school started asking me out for pizza with the gang after school, and before I knew it, I had boys calling me or coming over the house to take me to a football game or movie with friends. I was doing OK!

The Voice

My mom had a woman friend in the neighborhood that had a daughter who played an accordion for the Bridgeport Pal Band. She asked my mom if I would be interested in going for a singing audition. My mother told me we were going, and I went.

I was seventeen years old now. I went for the audition, and they liked me a lot. I had no idea that I would end up as their lead singer, sitting with the band and singing solo. I really enjoyed it. The only catch was that I had to march in the parades with the marching band. I started to go to the rehearsals, and it was a lot of work. We learned to compete with other marching bands and traveled around Connecticut and New York areas. I worked my way up to first lieutenant and won lots of awards.

I had many singing appearances. I sang for political events, business parties, and even went to a jail in upper Connecticut to sing for some of the prisoners. I had so many gigs for singing that I needed more material, and I had little time to rehearse.

My mother talked to some of the other moms who were sending their kids for lessons and decided to send me to a vocal coach. I think the only reason she was willing to put out the money was that she wanted to stay in the group of mothers herself. She was enjoying the traveling, and she even got to do a skit onstage with the other moms. She was tough with me even when I was so tired from school, color guard, and singing lessons; it didn't matter to her. Even when it was cold or snowy and school wasn't cancelled, she would make me get up and walk to school, which was a good mile and a half or more.

I was asked to open for a show at the Klein Memorial, which was a big thing back in those days. The Klein hosted many stars, which was a boost for the economy of Bridgeport. I had to look the part of course, so my mother took me to look for a gown. I remember how special it felt to be shopping for a gown! I finally chose a blue chiffon dress. It had little shoulder straps, and I felt like a star in it. I had the shoes dyed to match the gown, and I had a small crown with rhinestones on it.

I remember being so scared because if I didn't do well, I knew my mother would be a crazy person to me, especially since this was Bridgeport, where we lived. My father came to this event to see me perform, and he got a seat in the first row of the hall so I could see him. He came backstage to see me before I performed, and he could see red blotches on my neck and shoulders because I was so scared. He pulled out a small bottle of blackberry brandy and told me to take a little bit of it; I did. I guess nowadays that would be called abuse, but all I knew was that it helped, and when I went out onstage, I felt like I could sing my heart out. I did exactly that. I was great, and the applause from the audience said they loved me. I had a standing ovation.

After the Klein, word got out, and I was asked to sing at a huge field in upper Bridgeport. This was a field where a lot of concerts were held with some very big names. My job was to open that show for the guest star Jack Benny, the comedian who was the first star to perform. Well, I opened, and the number went off without a hitch. I nailed it for more than one reason. To be asked to open for the show was an honor, and also I wanted to make a good impression to Mr. Benny, who was the funniest person alive at that time. After the show was over, I rushed out to the parking area so I could at least say hello because I wasn't allowed to talk to Mr. Benny before the show started. I knew he would recognize me because he was standing offstage when I opened the show, and he looked at me as I passed him and went onstage. After the show, bodyguards rushed him to his limo. I got to the window of the limo and said hello to Mr. Benny, raised the paper and the pen to give it to him, and I started to say how happy I was to open the show for him. He looked at me with no expression on his face for a couple of seconds and just raised the window of the limo and took off. I thought my performance might have been bad, but it wasn't that at all. I was so disappointed. I wondered if all big stars acted like that, or maybe he just had a bad day.

One of my most memorable performances was when I sang at the Marriott Hotel in New York on Broadway. I studied the song "Wind Beneath My Wings" popularized by singer-actress Bette Midler. This appearance happened later in my career. I remember how excited I was to perform this number because it had a lot of meaning to me.

I guess I really never knew I was that good, but when the hotel staff started coming out of the kitchen and peeking around the doors to the ballroom, finally, I knew how it felt to capture the emotions of your audience.

It was from that point that I realized that all the studying and vocal coaching was the key to opening up and giving to your audience, and in turn, they gave something wonderful back to you.

My mother had a thing about sex, and every time I would go out with a boy, she acted mean to me like I was doing something wrong. If I was sitting on the porch, she would peek through the blinds and see what I was doing. My friends even noticed that she was kind of strange in that department. Why, I don't know. Catholic school teachings never left me, and I knew back then that if I did anything I shouldn't, I would surely die and go to hell.

I had met a very nice young boy from a Catholic high school through friends. He enjoyed coming over to my house and would talk to my dad. I liked him a lot. He was very smart and nice looking. John and I would go out on dates, like going for a ride to his house or going out to the movies with his friends from school and their girlfriends, sometimes going all together to picnics, things like that. One time, John and I went to the movies. Well, his car, believe it or not, actually had a flat tire. We were, needless to say, late in getting home to my house. My mother just reached over to me, slapped me in the face, and told him to go home. John had to call and apologize to my mom over and over again, or he knew that he wouldn't be able to see me ever again. Finally, with me begging my mother for weeks to let me see him again, she gave her permission.

During the time we were dating, I came down with a very bad case of bronchitis, which was getting worse by the day. John came over to the house with an electric blanket for my room. He knew how cold the back bedroom was, and I think he was concerned about how I was keeping warm. My dad thought that John bringing over the electric blanket was a very nice thing to do since the back bedroom was hard to heat with just the stove. My mother, on the other hand, did not like the idea very much.

John, the sweet boy I was dating, eventually had enough of my mother's constant questioning and crazy behavior. We broke up. It broke my heart, but I understood why. I never saw him again.

The Looking Glass

One Saturday, my girlfriends and I decided to go to a Saturday matinee at the American Theater. I had little time to myself with the singing, rehearsals, school, and a part-time job, so the idea of going to the movies was great. My mom worked a couple of hours on a Saturday, so I asked my dad if I could go with the girls, and he said OK!

I didn't pay much attention to the time; I was having fun. The movies back then were a couple of hours because those days, you got a cartoon and two movies compared to what we get now. The movie was over, and the girls and I started walking home. I could see Mr. Smith's car coming down the road with my mother in the backseat. It was then that I realized I was late for rehearsal at Pal. The car pulled over, and my mother got out, slapped me in the face, pulled my hair, threw me into the car, and started hitting me. Mrs. Smith, said, "Betty, stop! You are going to hurt her." She finally stopped, and I guess the Smiths finally got a true picture of her rage. My friends were so scared for me, they ran to my friend's house and told her mother that my mother was killing me.

It was then I decided to get out and leave home. The next couple of weeks, I asked my friend if her mother knew of any place I could stay. She told me about an Italian woman who had a room in her house in the north part of town. Bernice would have me stay with her, but they didn't have the room, and besides, I didn't want my mother to cause any problems for Bernice's mom. The day finally came. My mom was at work. I packed my clothes, called a cab, and left. I was still working part-time for Marianne's Clothing Store, so I could afford the rent for the room. I didn't have much. Any money I made while singing I never saw, but I knew I had to get away from my mom, whatever it took.

I called my father that night and told him that I wouldn't be coming home. I told him not to worry. I had a nice room near Saint Vincent's Hospital, and I asked him to meet with me on Saturday, and I would bring him to the house. He didn't say much; he just agreed to meet me. I told him that I couldn't bring him up to the room; no one was allowed—that was the rule that the Italian women who owned the house made very clear to me.

My father and I took the bus from downtown to the north side of town. The bus stopped in front of the hospital, and we walked down the street to the house. I introduced him to the owner, and she said we could sit on the bench in the downstairs hallway to visit. My dad, I guess, felt kind of assured that no one could come up to my room. He asked how I was going to pay for the room each week. I told him with the part-time job, I could possibly make it. And I would be graduating from school, and then I could get a full-time job. He went into his pocket and took out a twenty-dollar bill; it was a lot to me. He said he would visit me every weekend, and we could go out for lunch or something. I hugged him and told him I loved him.

I wondered why my mom never tried to even look me up or come and try to convince me to come home, but I guess I knew the reason why; I always knew the reason why.

One night, I got a knock on my door. The landlord told me that someone was in the hall downstairs and wanted to talk to me. It was Bernice and her mother. She said, "Liz, there was an accident at your dad's work, and he died at home." I went into shock. I started shaking. The earth fell under my feet. Bernice and her mom took me home to their house, and she called the doctor. I couldn't stop shaking and vomiting. I stayed the night, and then the next day, I went home. I thought that was the thing to do. My mom was as cold as ever to me. I felt so alone. The funeral lasted two days. It was the hardest time for me. After the funeral, I went back to my furnished room. I was never asked to stay at home. My sister managed to take everything that mattered to me; she even took a ring off my dad's hand before the burial. I was never given anything that belonged to him, not till years later did I find some little things of Dad's.

Graduation time came, and believe it or not, with everything going on, I got honors. To my surprise, my mom came to the graduation and told me to come back to the house for a small party. This was a major surprise; could it be that she had some feelings of love for me after all? I found out during the party that her friend, Joyce, convinced her to give me a little party. She told my mother, the other parents would think it strange of her if she didn't.

I went back to my room and started working full-time at the clothing store. Fall came and then winter. The room I had was an attic room, and it was cold. I wasn't allowed to cook, so I had a toaster and one of those things you plugged in the socket and put in a cup of water to make it hot; I don't remember what it was called. I was taking a bus to work every day and night. I couldn't afford a car or insurance. It was tough. The landlord decided to raise my rent, I guess to pay the oil bill, except I wasn't getting any heat. I was cold, hungry, and tired. I came down real sick, coughing and coughing. The landlady told me to go to the hospital down the street, and sure enough, I had pneumonia. They, right away, put me in a private room under strict supervision and care. They called my mother to let her know what was happening. I stayed in the hospital for,

I guess, seven days, and then I was released to my mother with instructions of care.

I stayed with my mom and eventually I got my strength back and then found a full-time job in a factory. I needed money. I had to pay her back for the hospital, and she wanted board and told me to buy my own food. The factory was the only paying job that would allow me to make the money I needed.

My mother now had a boyfriend who lived in New York and visited her on the weekends, he made it clear to me that he didn't like the idea that I was around. It was about two months after I moved in with my mother and I was watching television, he said to my mom, didn't she think it was time that I got out and find another place to live? She agreed with him and said that they needed to have time alone. I got the message. I found an apartment and moved out.

While I was working in the factory on an assembly line making electric shavers, which was a new experience for me, I kept on hearing that I was really pretty and why didn't I try to be a model? I realized that the factory was not a place for me when I had an experience where one of my coworkers reached across the assembly line and grabbed the girl on the other side by the neck. I thought she was going to kill her. I started to cry; I was so scared. The manager of the factory came down from the office to stop the argument and saw me crying. He said, "It's OK!" He asked me if I could type. I said, "Yes, a little." I guess he didn't think the assembly line was the place for me. He brought me up to the office, and he sat me down at a desk and handed me some files. That was the beginning of my new job as an office secretary.

My apartment was in a two-family house on the nicer side of Bridgeport, very close to the Beardsley Zoo. My landlord was a very nice man. One Sunday morning, he came over to inform me that he would be selling the house. He said to not worry about moving out because whoever bought the house would allow me to continue renting the apartment. I asked him how much he would be selling it for and asked if he would consider selling the house to me. He was very polite, telling me that he didn't think I could afford the down payment. He then said to me that if I could come up with the down payment in six months, he would consider selling it to me. I asked him how much the deposit would be. He said five thousand nine hundred dollars. That was a lot of money to me.

I figured that if I started modeling and worked two jobs that maybe, just maybe, I could come up with the money.

The fact that the house was a two family meant that the other rent could pay for the mortgage. I knew it wouldn't be easy, but I had to try!

Modeling

One Saturday, I was looking through the want ads, and I noticed an advertisement for Barbizon School of Modeling. I decided to give it a shot and go to one of their auditions in Stamford, Connecticut. After the audition, they offered me a spot in their training program. I was ecstatic. I thought if I could make some money modeling, it could help me raise the money for the down payment for the house. I went faithfully every Saturday morning on the train to class. The classes were involved in the many aspects of modeling. I had courses in model's presentation, fashion detail, makeup application, professional vocabulary, and resume preparation.

Our final grade average relied on our ability to put together an outfit of our own from head to toe with a minimum amount of money. We had to save our receipts and spend no more than the allowed amount, $50.

I went to all the discount stores to purchase clothing and accessories, which were important to the final fashion look.

The combination of accessories had to be balanced with the main outfit, whether it was a dress, suit, pants, or whatever. I also performed a skit. The skit was a known commercial at that time and was seen often on television. It was about a woman who was a mother and who worked. It was kind of a funny takeoff of how much a woman can do. I came on stage with an oversized, long bathrobe and a hairnet with rollers as I sang the lyrics. When the lyrics said "bring home the bacon," I took off the hairnet and robe, and I was dressed in a form-fitting dress with high heels and acted like a hot dish myself. I got a round of applause from the audience; I guess they liked it!

After I graduated from the program, I was offered several different modeling assignments for major department stores and advertisements. I modeled for Diane von Furstenberg, Catalina Sports, Lord & Taylor, Macy's, hair salons, and fashion shows.

The six months were tough. I worked full-time at the factory, part-time from six to ten in the evenings for a meat-packing company as a router for deliveries for the following day, and the modeling on the weekends.

I sacrificed as much as I could; after all, that was nothing new to me. My icebox had a head of lettuce, tomatoes, some chicken when I could afford it, and cans and cans of tuna. I walked when I could instead of taking the bus to save money. I just wanted to have something I could call my own and create a new life for myself.

The six months came, and I did it! I walked into my landlord's office and handed him a bank check for the deposit. He said he was really surprised, and he gave me a lot of credit. I was so happy and so proud. I now was a property owner, and I was, after all, only twenty years old.

There were a lot of difficult times in the beginning of my career. I once came to meet an agent and his wife through another business acquaintance. The agent had an office in Manhattan. His wife was a lovely woman, very polished. He seemed very businesslike and, I thought, well liked. I found out later that his wife was what kept him from ruin.

We seemed to have a lot in common, and at this point, I was starting up my own clientele. I asked him if we could get together to discuss some business ideas. I made an appointment and went into the city to see him.

When I got to the office, he was very glad to see me and mentioned how hot it was. It was the middle of July, and the city was like a slow cooker, hotter than hell! He offered me some cold iced tea, and we began our conversation. It was about an hour when we finally started talking about contracts and the legal side of clients' rights.

Then all of a sudden, he grabbed my leg; I had been sitting on the side of the desk. I thought, *What is he doing?* He took off my shoe and said that my feet must be killing me after walking from the train station. I pulled my leg back, and he reached for it again. I said, "Tom, I feel just fine." He pulled back on my leg, and I jumped up, grabbed my shoe, and said, "What is *wrong* with you?" He said nothing and just smiled. I said, "I think this appointment is over." I later learned that he had a foot fetish, and it was kept quiet because of his wife. I guess now that I look back on it, it was kind of funny, sort of like a comedy skit if it wasn't so real.

I remember an incident with a photographer. I was doing a shoot for a noted hair salon magazine. The hairstylist was at the studio and did my hair in a very glamorous style. When the stylist left the studio, the photographer led me to a screen in the corner of the room where I was to change. The hair salon requested that I wear a gown for the shoot. I was a little uneasy about changing there, and I wondered why he didn't have a real dressing room to change in. I didn't want to appear naive, and I was getting a nice amount of money for the booking, so I acted like it was no problem at all. The photographer asked me how I was doing. I said, "OK!" And I went out for my first shot. He was very polite and seemed professional, so I started to feel comfortable with him, and he mentioned how beautiful the shots were looking. The session lasted about forty-five minutes to an hour, and he said it was a take.

I went to change, and before I knew it, I turned around, and he was standing at the edge of the screen, looking at me changing. I was in my bra and panties, and he looked at me and asked if he could help. I was shocked. I grabbed my gown and tried to cover myself and said, "I am doing just fine." He approached me, and I screamed as loud as I could. He backed off and said, "I was only trying to help. You're not going to say anything to any body about this, are you?" I said, "Just leave me alone." I got dressed and left the studio as quickly as I could. I never told anyone about the incident. I just became a little wiser and a lot less naive.

There was a TV talk show host in New York City who I heard about and who gave newcomers a chance to get into the business. I decided that, with my singing background and the modeling, I could possibly get some exposure in this talk show.

I sent my photo and resume to him, and I did manage to get an appointment. I knocked on the door of his office, and when he opened the door, he seemed annoyed that I had brought my assistant with me. He asked me to tell my assistant to wait outside. I entered the room; it was filled with books, photos, and records from wall to wall. The only visible spot was a large couch and a desk in the corner of the room. He seemed very sharp with me and didn't look interested in even talking to me now. It was clear that he didn't like the idea of having my assistant sitting outside of the door. He looked at my photo again and said the he had another appointment and the interview had to be cut short, which seemed strange to me because when we spoke over the phone, he said the appointment would take at least forty-five minutes to an hour. He started to lead me to the door, and before he opened the door, he said, "You should really grow up if you want to make it in this business." I guess he had some other ideas about my interview, that was made very clear to me.

There were other times that things didn't turn out the way I thought they would. I heard of a recording studio in downtown Bridgeport that was looking for background singers, so I called the studio. They asked me to send a photo and a resume, and they would get back to me. That wasn't unusual because that was how things were done. This seemed like it was a professional situation. I got a call about two weeks after I sent the photo, and they made an appointment with me; I was so excited!

I got to the studio. It was located on the third floor of a building complex. Downtown Bridgeport back then, believe it or not, was not such a bad place. The office had a very nice waiting room, and I could see and hear music coming from the recording studios in the office. The receptionist called in and let the owner know that I was there. This very good-looking man came out into the waiting room and asked me to come into his office. The office was done very nicely. While he was looking over my head shot and resume, another man came into the office; he was probably in his late thirties. He sat on a corner chair and listened as I spoke to the other man. The older man in the corner asked me how old I was, where I lived, and if I was living at home with my parents. I answered his questions. He got up and went over to the desk. He leaned on the desk and looked at the other man sitting behind the desk. He said to him, "I think this young woman is beautiful, don't you?" The other man said, "Yes, she is lovely." The older man said, "Give her the job." Then he left the room. I asked, "Didn't he want to hear me sing? Don't you want to hear me sing?" He said, "If the boss says you got the job, I guess you got it."

I left the office and wasn't quite sure what was going on. I talked to a friend of mine and her older sister, Joyce. She said, "Liz, this doesn't sound right to me." I agreed with her. She asked a few friends she knew around town to check into this studio.

Well, it turned out that the same owner of the so-called recording studio also had an escort and stripper business. I never went back to that studio, and they called me at least three times. I learned that having good looks back then was not everything it was cracked up to be.

I finally got an agent in New York whom I felt I could trust. I liked her, and she gave me some really great bookings. She understood who I was and made sure I wasn't put in any compromising situations. I modeled for Lord & Taylor, Catalina Sportswear, Gloria Vanderbilt designs and introduced her wraparound dress, J. C. Penney's, newspaper advertisements, and numerous fashion shows. I also did a lot of print work for hair salons, like John Samuels, Fine Arts of Stratford, Fontainebleau, and lots of work for clothing boutiques.

Yvonne was my manager for a year, and then because of some health issues, I believe she decided to leave the business. I was very upset, but I understood. I for one could certainly appreciate that our lives take many roads, and we have to accept those changes when they happen.

**Monday to Thursday Only
At Any Of The Following Super Salons**

JOHN & SAMUELS
1202 Main St., Bpt. 336-3181

SHOPPERS BEAUTY SALON
Shoppers Fair Plaza, Bpt. 335-5866

FINE ARTS OF STRATFORD
2896 Main St., Stratford 378-8808

FONTAINE BLEAU
Compo Shopping Cntr., W'spt. 227-0058

Liz

Liz

Promotion for Hair Salons
Liz

Fashion Shoot
Liz

Model Shoots
Promotion for Boots
Liz

The Business

I decided to try to open my own business. I had five hundred dollars in my pocket and was determined to find an office and make it work. A business that was a legit place where you could trust the agent or manager to do the best for you. A place where a parent of a child or an adult actor could feel comfortable and know they were in responsible hands.

I was determined to find an office and make it work. I knew I would need more capital, but I thought, *If I could just find the right place, I could work it all out.*

One day, I was driving through the town of Stratford. I noticed a business building under construction being raised a few levels. It had a few businesses on the first floor, and I saw a very handsome man in a police uniform standing on the top of the roof. I stopped the car and yelled up to the man and asked if he owned the building. He said he did, and asked, "What can I help you with?" I asked him if he would be renting out the new spaces, and he said he would, but it wouldn't be for at least a couple of months. I told him that I was interested. He came down from the building and gave me his number, and I gave him mine. He said he would call when the building was ready. He said if it worked out that I was going to rent an office space, he would need a month's rent and a month's security.

I knew I had to get more cash right away. I went to a local bank and got a personal loan for twenty-five hundred dollars.

I finally got the appointment to see the layout of the office space. He asked me what the business was going to be, and I told him I was a professional actor, singer, and model and that I would be opening a legit management/casting office.

I decided to have a small waiting room and a larger room for interviewing. The price was right, and that was what I could afford at the time.

I finally moved into the office. I went to all the cheap stores I could find to get chairs and table lamps. I even went to consignment stores. I got a glass dining room table and turned it into a desk; it really looked classy, and I decorated the walls with Broadway signs and mirrors. I had a long upright file cabinet. My phone and I was ready to go!

I started making calls to everyone I had contacts with, and the ball started rolling. I had an open house and hired two young girls to hand out balloons. I couldn't believe how many people came to the open house. It was great!

The clients started signing up for information sessions. I even had a mother from one of the local schools ask if I would come in to put on a little play with the children. Of course, I said yes; I loved it. It didn't take long before another school called and asked me to teach some dance exercises at their school. I was busy. I decided to hire two instructors to teach exercise classes. I also rented another room adjoining my office and enlarged my space to hold exercise classes in the office next to my private office.

The calls from New York City were coming in for movies, commercials, and TV series, and stores were calling for catalogue work. I hired, within the first year, a staff of five assistants.

I realized that I should get my degree in business administration, especially running my own business. I followed up on getting into Housatonic Community College. I thought if I could get at least some credit there, I could finish my degree in another university. I went three nights a week after work, taking as many courses as I possibly could.

I loved college; it was such a melting ground for new ideas and various opinions.

My professors were very down-to-earth and taught their classes with a sense of ease that made learning a joy. I did very well and had a great point average. It would be some time before I could finish my degree, but I started, and I was happy with what I achieved.

My business involved giving one-to-one advisement sessions to prospective clients. I would advise them on auditions, including how to approach the interviewer to make sure they demonstrated a positive behavior and knowledge about the part they were auditioning for. Research was always the key. I advised them on the tools necessary for the audition. The head shot was always necessary, videos of past performances, and monologues—at least two, one being drama and the other one lighthearted or comedy. Cold readings should be treated as naturally as possible.

The appearance of an actor was always a concern when going for an audition. I suggested that the actor perhaps wear something in their wardrobe that reflected the part they were auditioning for. If the part was for a doctor, that they wear a shirt and a jacket. If the part was for a nurse, that they included a white shirt or dress in their wardrobe. If auditioning as a rock band leader, he should have a bandana around his head and some large pieces of jewelry. This would give the casting panel a bird's-eye view of how this actor would look on a set. I always told my actors that a smile and a great personality would be better than going in with an attitude. The casting agent wants to know that they can work with the actor easily and reasonably.

One of my client's trailer on set for <u>Great Expectations</u>

This is a typical compartment or Woodshed as it has been called of a trailer with other private compartments that is on site when a Movie or a series is being shot.

The private compartment has a vanity and sink with a mirror. A private toilet and a resting area for the actor to use during takes or just to have time to study their lines as I have done many times.

The trailer also can have make-up and wardrobe compartments.

Their resume, if possible, should include multiple activities like bike riding, swimming, pool playing, and race car driving. These things would widen their chances for more various types of jobs. I always advised multilanguages, if possible, also be listed on the resume.

Children, on the other hand, should be treated much differently than adults. I once had a child come in the office with his mother. He was really cute with big blue eyes and a beautiful full head of jet-black hair. He really was quite adorable. I addressed my questions to the mother. I asked her why she felt that her son would be interested in acting or modeling. She started telling me how he loved watching Disney channels and how he would imitate other characters he saw on the television.

I then decided to direct my questions to the little boy. I asked him if he would like to be on a Disney show on TV. He said *no*! I asked him if he knew why he was here. He said *no*! I asked him if he wanted to have his picture taken. He said *no*! I tried to get him to talk to me and feel relaxed. I even gave him a game to play with. I spent at least one hour trying to make him comfortable. Nothing worked. I finally asked him if he wanted to go home. He said *yes*! But he wanted to go for his ice cream that his mommy promised him after the audition.

I said to his mom, "He is nicely telling us he isn't interested." She replied, "He will do what I tell him to do." I told her,

"That wouldn't work here in this office." I said the interview was over, and she left in a hurry.

Patrick Dempsey, myself, and my clients in the
very beginning before he became famous.
28 years ago 1983 – 1984

Patrick Dempsey, now recognized as Mr. McDreamy in Grey's Anatomy, *the TV series. He was spotted at a talent showcase in NY with his sparkling eyes and a great big smile. The photo is of Patrick before he became a star with two of my clients and myself.*

My business introduced me to many talent agencies. I had received information about a company called Talent America that was located in Providence, Rhode Island.

I found the concept of that particular company interesting. I contacted the owner, Jayne Eastwood.

We agreed, after an in-depth phone conversation, to meet.

We finally got together, and I found that our interests were similar. We both wanted to give our clients the most exposure to the entertainment industry as possible. It was funny because Jayne was checking me out as I was her. We laugh about it even now.

Mrs. Eastwood's business revolved around a talent showcase, a place where the most talented could perform in front of noted agents and managers after being selected at previous other preliminaries. The final showcase was held in New York and Stamford, Connecticut.

I was asked if I would consider becoming an area director who would arrange preliminary showcases in the Connecticut area. Those individuals who showed potential were asked to perform again in New York City. I was delighted to do so. It turned out to be a wonderful experience for myself as well as my clients.

There was one time, however, that the showcase was scheduled shortly after the first attempt on the Trade Towers in New York City. Many of the contestants were scared that another would be made while they were there.

I was asked to participate as an MC for the showcase, and I could sense the tension. I got up and started singing "God

Bless America" onstage, and everyone started singing with me. The kids started making a waving motion with hands held high, and tears started running down my face. I was exactly what everyone needed. I was so happy that I could give them a little bit of joy and hope.

Ruth Ann,
one of my clients who was cast for Les Miserables on tour

Myself and one of my Child models receiving an award for modeling.

Trade Towers, NY

Jane Eastwood
President of Talent America and a dear friend for over 28 years.
With Erna La Plume
A smart, classy and funny lady

Receiving an award from Talent America for the "Director of the Year Award"

My exercise staff for my business. Dressed in purple black.

One of the routines I directed for my talent showcase.
New York, NY

The Unexpected

One day, as usual, I was interviewing new prospective clients when this young man in his late twenties walked into the office. He wanted to be a model; there was something about him that I found intriguing. His name was Sal. I knew that he was too short to be a runway model and, at that time, too ethnic, but I knew that I couldn't let him go out of the office, never to see him again. I offered him the opportunity to work with me as I did for those clients who I felt had the ability to work in the business. I didn't know what was going to happen, but I knew that I had to keep this man in my sight.

I offered an exercise program for my clients to help keep them in shape. I hired two young women who were certified in aerobic training, and we had classes twice a week.

I usually would join in with the classes if I didn't have appointments. One night, my instructor couldn't make it to class, so I had to fill in. I put on my tights and went out to teach the class, and in the corner of the room, there he was, Sal, his eyes piercing as though he could see through me. I tried to pay attention to the music and the exercise, but I couldn't help glancing over to the corner of the room. After that night, I knew something was happening that we had no control with. Every time we were in the same room, the sexual tension was there.

Aspiring to a dream

(Continued from C 1)

"Don't sit in the corner. Walk up to the person who is interviewing you and shake their hand. Stay informed. Interject your views in a conversation. Let people know you have brains. In other words, make a good impression they will remember," coaches Lis.

Lis maintains contacts with New York City agencies and cosmetic companies and advises her students and their families to have a realistic view of their chances for success. For example, women who stands less than 5'8" tall would be passed over in high fashion modeling as would men under 6 feet and people in their late twenties or older.

However, there is a place for models doing catalogue layouts, product promotions in department stores and shopping malls, trade shows, charity events and commericials. A new category for models was recently created called petite modeling for women who are about 5'2".

Telling her students how to avoid the questionable side of the business, she warns them to refuse to sign any agreements until they know where the photos will appear, living within their means (she recommends investing the money) and most of all, not doing anything that would bother their consciences later. Raised by parents who immigrated from Ireland, Lis refused to be photographed in bathing suits, modeling only Catalina's blouses and wrap around skirts.

What makes modeling such hard work? There is the constant threat of rejection and the pursuit of perfection, the long hours, perhaps under very hot lights, sometimes in clothes that are fastened with jabbing pins, and the likelihood of long commutes on the train or in tied up traffic jams.

In order to maintain that pace and a weight that is five to eight pounds below the minimum standards recommended by health professionals, Lis provides diet counseling. A nurse who is just a couple of semesters shy of a doctorate in psychology, she worked with Dr. Virginia Blank in Fairfield before opening the Health and Beauty Workshop two years ago. During the first month of the training, Lis instructs all students to keep logs of what and when they eat so she can be sure they are maintaining sound eating habits. She is aware that eating disorders like anorexia and bulimia require special attention.

As Lis talks about her goals, she looks forward to acquiring a larger facility, one that will include a photographic studio. Also, she would like to train more mature women who have always dreamed of modeling, but thought the possibility ended with the first whisper of a wrinkle or strand of gray. That is no longer true says Lis.

The Unexpected

I decided to put on a review for all my clients. I called in all my contacts, every agent I knew, photographers, and anyone else I could think of for exposure.

I directed and taught all the routines myself and called in a fashion boutique to help with the modeling aspect of the review. One of the skits was from the review *Grease*, the movie with John Travolta and Olivia. The scene we did was when Olivia decided to change her look and try to seduce her way into Tony's heart. In the movie, Olivia wore a black leather jumpsuit that was tight and sexy. The two clients that I was teaching the routine to didn't quite get the feel of the dance, so I asked if anyone from the cast would like to show them what I was talking about. The hand went up. Guess who's hand—it was Sal. I said, "Great, come over here." And I asked if any one of the female clients were interested in coming up. I was hoping that someone would volunteer; nobody did, so I had to step in. Sal came toward me. I tried to maintain a professional attitude. Sal put his arm around my waist, drew me close, and I felt the heat between us as we swayed to the music back and forth, and the room went quiet. I could feel the eyes of my clients on us, and no one spoke a word. I could feel my face turn red, and we kept on moving back and forth to the music like we were making love right in front of everyone in the room.

The relationship between Sal and myself needless to say grew quickly. Sal told me he was going to Florida to see his daughter. I was amazed he had a daughter! I had said I would go out with him after he came back from his trip, but now, I was wondering if that was a good idea. I guess time would tell.

I had decided to go for a trip myself with a young woman in the same office complex, who I had gotten to know as a business friend. We had gone out to lunch and other special events, which we had gone to for business contacts.

We decided to go to the islands for a short getaway. We had a great time going shopping and, at night, visiting the social life. I couldn't help wondering during the trip how the first date with Sal would work out, and I wondered about his daughter. What was that all about?

Sal and I had gotten back from our trips, and sure enough, he was right there, making arrangements for our first date. We decided to go to a local restaurant where there was dancing. I dressed in a sexy little number: a black-and-red off-shoulder dress with red high heels. I was very confident that I looked great.

We danced the night away. Sal was not the greatest dancer, but he tried. The vibrations between us were intense. It didn't matter that he couldn't dance; his eyes pierced me like he could see my very soul. He could see a desire in me that I always knew was there, but had never been aroused with such fury.

We ended the night and went out to the car in the parking lot. He reached to kiss me, and my response was so intense that I felt that I was not in control of my emotions. I kissed him back with such burning passion that it made him draw back, trying to control himself. He took one long breath and said, "We should stop." I was totally surprised, but he was right. It wasn't the right time, and he dropped me home.

In time, Sal and I grew closer and closer, and a true love arose between us. This man would be the love of my life. We had many family gatherings with Sal's parents and brothers. They were a true Italian family. I think the one thing that was attractive to me was the idea of a real family to share holidays with and have large family get-togethers. Sal had three older brothers and so many cousins; I couldn't even count them all. I thought I was starting the perfect family life, but as you know, nothing is quite as perfect as you would like. It takes a lot of work to be a family member. The differences with certain nationalities can sometimes be a difficult situation to deal with. What did I know about the Italian dish, pasta? I was an Irish girl who ate meat and potatoes. Trying to understand another human being is often hard, but eventually, it can be achieved. You can, believe it or not, even make a reasonable version of a pasta dish.

I will never forget the first time I met Sal's daughter. He had brought her into my office one day after his trip to Florida.

She had long straight blonde hair. She was a tiny little thing but with these beautiful brown longing eyes.

Sal had told me he was taking full custody of her and that they would be living with his mom at her house. I wasn't sure how I would feel if Sal and I got serious about staying together and becoming a mother right after I said, "I do!"

Sal and I made a point of spending as much time alone as we could so that we got to know each other. We also made a point of spending time with his daughter on the weekends, going to the park and taking long rides, doing a lot of things that kids like to do.

It wasn't long before she started calling me Mom. This little bundle of energy was a complete joy to me. The first big shopping day was a special experience. I learned that this little girl had a style all her own.

I would go over to Sal's house sometimes during the week after work and make it just in time to tuck her into bed.

She was always asking if she could be a model. I decided to let her try some runway modeling to see if she really liked it.

I was judging a model pageant in Rhode Island. I had bought a beautiful pink gown for her to wear. She looked beautiful, and she did such a great job with her model routine, which we had practiced. She came down from the runway after her performance and stood by my side. She looked at me as if she had something to say, and I bent over to listen. She whispered into my ear, "Do I have to do this? It isn't what I thought it would be." The memory of my childhood flashed through my mind, and I said, "No! You can do what makes you happy." Then, she told me she wanted to work with animals. If that was her dream, I was going to help her make it happen.

I had learned from my experience as a child that it is important for a child to feel worth in what they do, and the job of a parent is to instill those feelings of worth by always finding the child's strengths and building upon them. I promised myself that I would be a good mom and never let her go through what I had as a child.

Sal, his daughter, and I became a family. We decided it was time to make our own home together. We were married in a year and a half and started our new lives together.

Liz Tobin, owner of LT's Talent and Model Management, poses with three of her clients, left to right, Danica Zold, Suzanne Curry and Jason Calabrese.

Connecticut Post/David O. Gunn

Finding talent is a talent for Seymour firm

By MARY BETH NELSEN
Correspondent

SEYMOUR — Liz Tobin of LT's Model and Talent Management would love to change the negative image of talent managers.

"I know there are stereotypical pushy managers out there, especially with children," Tobin said. "It doesn't have to be like that. Don't work with someone who makes you feel uncomfortable. Go with your gut."

Tobin ought to know. Once a child actress herself, she strives to make her youngest clients comfortable in a business that can be tough, demanding and hard on the ego.

"When a parent comes in, I make time to speak to the child alone. I want to be sure they understand what this is all about. I ask them 'why are you here.' If the answer is 'my mom said so,' well then, maybe this isn't the right thing for that child. But if the child gets all excited about wanting to perform and sing and dance and be on Broadway, that's a very different scenario."

Tobin either gets her clients through referrals or from the hundreds of photos and résumés that come across her desk. When she agrees to take on a new client, Tobin starts with some advice.

"I'll recommend what I think will benefit them — voice, dance lessons, acting classes. I encourage my clients to act in local theater, too. It's important to build that portfolio."

She emphasized that getting into the business doesn't require expensive photos or the services of a "management group" that promises stardom in return for a large chunk of cash.

It requires talent and the willingness to develop one's skills, she said.

On Mondays Tobin is in New York City, maintaining the contacts she has developed during the past 16 years, and scouting for opportunities.

Talent manager Liz Tobin sits in her Seymour office of LT's Model and Talent Management.

Scott Biglietti/For the Connecticut Post

The rest of the week she's in her Seymour office working with clients, setting up auditions and jobs with her assistant, Michelle Musante.

Tobin moved her business from Fairfield about two years ago to escape the rush hour traffic, and finds the Valley a great place to work.

The client list ranges from age 6 to .. "well, we have guys who can play Santa."

She strives to maintain a group of clients who can meet the needs of casting directors.

Her clients have worked in industrial and educational videos and television. They have done print work for Foxwoods and Mohegan Sun casinos, *Reader's Digest*, *Seventeen* and *Glamour* magazines, and have appeared in movies, including "Sleepers" and "Other People's Money."

Recently, Tobin arranged to have a bus pick up a group of child clients who are working in an upcoming movie starring Susan Sarandon and Julia Roberts called "Goodbye, Moon."

"People were amazed that I had the nerve to ask for a bus," Tobin said. Tobin takes pains to give casting directors exactly what they want.

"That's why we work. A good percentage of my clients land the job. Neither their time nor the casting director's time is wasted. Sometimes the audition involves a trip to [New York City] or a half-day missed from work or school, so it's important to send people on worthwhile auditions," Tobin said.

Tobin, a performer since childhood, understands her client's experiences. She stills sings at the Marriott Marquis in New York City, and remains active in drama — well, maybe not exactly "active." Her most recent role was as a corpse on television's "Law and Order."

"The hardest thing was, I had to audition," she said.

Sal's mom and dad at one of our family gatherings.

The Irish side of the family getting together
Myself with cousins in Ireland

Sal's daughter and myself

Shauna and myself in front of the statue of Mary at St. Michael's Church in Derby, CT

Sal and I married starting a family

Hollywood

When I first started up the business, one of the first major movies I was asked to cast for was *Sleepers*.

If you remember the movie, it was about young boys in a reformatory who were abused by the guards. One guard was played by Kevin Bacon. His character in the script was, by far, extremely vindictive. The script called for young boys between eight to twelve years old and of all races.

I had the opportunity to cast about twenty young boys for the scene. The movie, a good portion of it, was shot at Fairfield Hills in Connecticut. The hospital was, at one time, for mentally ill patients and had been abandoned for quite some time. The shooting of the movie was quite an experience for my young clients.

The story ended with those young boys who made it through and survived the ordeal in the reformatory and who are now young men, and for the most part, accomplishing their goals in life except to make the guard at the reformatory pay for what he did to them as children. They decided to reach out to a catholic priest played by Robert De Niro, whom the young men went to for solace. The movie, when it came out, was a hit.

The business gave me the opportunity to act on many of the sets that my clients were booked on. I had my first role as the Mayor's Receptionist in the movie *Whispers of White*. It was a movie about corrupt cops and gangsters who were selling and shipping coke to different cities in the United States. It was shot in Bridgeport, Connecticut, in the town hall in the mayor's office. I had been casting the movie for my clients, and while I was on set, the director asked me to play the part of the receptionist. I told him that I was acting as a casting agent for my clients, and he said that it didn't matter to him. He thought I would be just right for the role. My lines were very short. I was acting as the Mayor's Receptionist, and all I had to say was, "The mayor will see you now." Whatever happened to that movie, I will never know. If you have ever acted, you know for even the smallest part or speaking lines, you think out how the lines should be said. I did exactly that. For instance, should I be serious? Should I act like a dippy kind of receptionist? Do I have an accent? And so on and so on and so on.

I also had the opportunity to work on *Law and Order* as the woman Laura Matson, a Wall Street executive who is knocked off by her husband and stepdaughter. The episode was called "Family Values." One of the scenes took place on the East River in New York City. I remember it as the coldest day in the month of June. I was put in a basket that the police put victims in when they drag them out of the river. They wet me down as if I had been in the water for several days. Before the shoot actually took place, I was in the trailer, having makeup applied. I had the opportunity to meet Jerry Orbach, sitting to my left in his makeup chair. His character was Lennie Briscoe, and Chris North was sitting to the right of me, having his makeup applied. Jerry played one of the detectives on the show for years. He was very nice and pleasant to talk with. He had a smile as big as he was tall. I could tell he was liked by everyone on set. He made the whole experience a pleasant one. We laughed and talked about my business and the business in general. The makeup artist applied makeup that made me look like a real dead person. The funny thing about it was that after the van dropped me off, I had to walk to our mark under the bridge, and while I was walking, I saw a bum who was leaning against a pole, drinking from a bottle in a paper bag. When he took a look at me with all the makeup on, I guess he thought he really did see a ghost. He dropped the bag and took off running down the street.

The list of movies I casted for were many. My clients were kept busy both as principal and extra actors along with being body doubles and stand-ins. Some other projects worked on were *Jason* the horror film; *Devil*; also *Devil's House*; *Sisterhood of the Traveling Pants*; *Other People's Money* with Danny DeVito, which was partially shot in Seymour, Connecticut; *Money Train*; *Great Expectations*; *Bronx Is Burning* with John Turturro, shot at ESPN in Connecticut; *Scenes from a Mall* with Bette Midler; *Long Time Nothing New*; *Revolutionary Road* with Leonardo DiCaprio, which was shot in Beacon Falls; and *Eddie* with Whoopi Goldberg.

We also cast for industrials such as People's Savings Bank, United Postal Services, FedEx, SNET. We also did a very interesting industrial for a company to show the horrors of terrorism. The shoot took place in a mall where the people going about shopping or having some fun eating were confronted with a terrorist attack. The actors who portrayed mothers, children, and fathers actually responded as a real victim might. This video was distributed as a training video to show how a terrorist attack could affect the general population.

We also did casting for videos and educational videos. One educational video we were asked to cast for was titled *Hazing and Harassment*. Which some of my actors had personally experienced. The video centered on the horrible things that the person had to endure while the hazing took place, usually in college or even in high school. This video was very sensitive for me because of my experiences as a child. Bullying is a form of harassment that can leave scars for many years on the person who has to endure the cruelty. The video is seen by educational institutes to help enlighten students to the realistic side of this treatment.

One movie that really got my attention was a movie entitled *Killer*. The main character was played by James Woods. The storyline was about a serial killer who couldn't stop his impulse to kill especially women.

I was asked to cast some extras for the movie that was shot in Connecticut, my home state. I had about twenty actors in a courtroom scene. I went along with the actors since it was not far from my office. While I was in the holding room, the director came over to me and asked if I would play the stenographer in the courtroom scene. He said that the scene involved me dressing in a period outfit. I said, "Why not!"

James Woods and myself on the set of the movie Killer

I soon found out that the period of time he was talking about was when women of that profession were very plain and wore dark stockings, no makeup, hair pulled back, and wore a corset.

The time came for me to leave the makeup room and report to the holding room until I was asked to come on set. I walked past some of my clients, and not one recognized me. I guess this was one way of expressing to my clients that acting is the ability to come out of you and become that character that the storyline depicts. Believe me when I say that many stars could possibly not even be recognized on the street when not in costume or character.

The shoot went well, and I never realized just how ingenious Mr. Woods was as an actor. He had a lot of input with the dialogue, and he knew exactly how to come across. After a couple of takes, Mr. Woods and myself started talking, and he requested that the staff take a snapshot of us together and gave the photo to me. We talked and ended up doing the Charleston on set, having some fun.

Local actors have a second mother fighting for roles

BY QUANNAH LEONARD
REPUBLICAN-AMERICAN

BEACON FALLS — Some of Liz Tobin Falzone's modeling and acting clients consider her a second mom.

Tobin, of Lasky Road, has been operating a modeling and acting management business for 25 years. Like a good mom, she's fighting to get local talent noticed by companies filming productions in Connecticut.

Earlier this year, the state enacted a tax-incentive program for companies filming movies or other productions in Connecticut. Effective as of July, it began giving tax credits of up to 30 percent on motion picture costs exceeding $50,000.

sure school came first, said Kekacs, who was an extra in "War of the Worlds."

"She is like a second mom," Kekacs said. "She honestly is. I grew up with her. She is very compassionate."

Markanthony Izzo, 48, of Derby, another Tobin client, said the tax credit program will be a good thing for Connecticut, especially for local talent.

"We're looking to get more work," said Izzo.

> "EVERY DAY IS A NEW ADVENTURE. I LOVE WATCHING THE PEOPLE. I LOVE WATCHING THEM GROW AND MATURE."

War of the Worlds

For *War of the Worlds*, I was called by an agent in California who was working directly with Mr. Spielberg and wanted me to provide for him extras for the movie. He told me that the location for this particular scene was in Naugatuck, Connecticut, at the old Uniroyal factory, which was only about fifteen minutes from my hometown. I couldn't pass up the opportunity to provide some jobs to my clients who lived in the valley. He asked for about thirty-five extras, and I gladly assisted him. My clients were excited to be given the chance to work with Mr. Spielberg and to have a chance to work close to home without traveling to the city for work.

Billy, the agent, was happy that I got him the extras that were needed, and he asked me if I would be coming with the actors. I said that I would love to meet him as we had worked together on another project but had never met in person. I said that I would be there with my clients on set at five in the morning. I met my clients that morning in the parking lot of the old factory, which had been shut down for quite a long time. It was the source of income for many residents of Naugatuck and was considered a piece of history.

The factory was chosen because it had that battled look and it could easily be accessed by the actors, but yet closed off for the privacy of the shoot. The local police provided security, and no one could get into the set unless their name was on the list of actors, the "call list."

The crew was very professional; the makeup and wardrobe people did a great job with making you look like you were really in a battle. One of my clients, Angelo, had the whole side of his face made up to look like it had been blown off and disfigured. It looked extremely realistic.

The scenes were filled with lots of energy—running away from the aliens, hiding behind buildings, and lots of screams. One of the scenes was when the people were hiding in a tunnel to escape the aliens. Tom Cruise was hiding in the tunnel with the actors, and when the time came to run away, my client, Sara, slipped on the wet pavement and went down. Tom right away rushed over to her, helped her up, and made sure she was all right. He was very attentive and caring. I am sure to this day that Sara still remembers the incident.

I had the opportunity to speak to Mr. Spielberg personally during one of the shoots. I decided if my clients were going to get dressed up in old torn clothes and have dirt put on their faces that I would do the same. When Billy, the casting director, asked me if I wanted to join my clients on set, I said, "Why not?" And it was during a particular scene that Mr. Spielberg approached me and asked in a joking way how I was enjoying being a beat-up woman from Wall Street in my torn clothes and dirt on my face. I told him it wasn't bad. He thanked me for all the actors on set and mentioned how professional they all were. He had a really nice smile and was very friendly, although when it came down to business, he expected professionalism from everyone on his crew, and I got the feeling that everyone who worked with him appreciated that attitude.

Sara's fall wasn't the only incident we had. In one of the scenes near the railroad tracks, I was running away from the aliens with my clients and other actors. The actor in front of us tripped on the railroad track and a domino effect started, and down I went with everybody else. I ended up spraining my ankle. The crew picked me up, put me in a van, and took me to Bridgeport Hospital. As I was put in the wheelchair, I could sense the nurses backing off from me a little. I really couldn't blame them. I really looked like a homeless person and my clothes were not the cleanest. After the doctor looked at my ankle and told me it was just a sprain, I called my husband to pick me up. When he arrived at the hospital, he looked in the exam room and not recognizing me, passed right by. I had to call out to him, "Sal, it's Liz!" I ended up putting some ice on the sprain that night and was back on the set faithfully the next day.

Extras recall 'awesome time' on set of Spielberg's

By KATE RAMUNNI
Correspondent

SEYMOUR — They spent two days shivering in the bitter cold, decked out in makeup and performing tasks that got several of them injured.

But it was two days they will never forget, and would do over in a heartbeat, several of the extras in the new Stephen Spielberg film, "War of the Worlds," said Friday.

Several dozen of those involved gathered before a showing of the film Friday evening at the Entertainment Cinemas to relive the experience.

"It was cold," Robert Niebrzydowski, 33, of Waterbury, said. "But every single minute was worth it."

Spielberg hired about 35 extras for the film through the L.T. Modeling and Talent Agency in Beacon Falls for the filming that took place at the old Uniroyal factory in Naugatuck.

They spent two days, just after Thanksgiving, filming one of the film's final battle scenes in bitterly cold temperatures.

"It was amazing being in the presence of such greats as Spielberg," Tiwanna Lewis of East Hartford said. "I had an awesome time."

For 19-year-old Sara Kekacs of Oxford, it was an opportunity to land in the arms of Tom Cruise.

Kekacs, an architecture student at the University of New Haven, has her hopes set on Hollywood.

In addition to "War of the Worlds," she also has appeared in the movies "Stepmom" and "The Object of My Affection."

"I was running through a tunnel up a very big incline, and just as I reached the top Stephen Spielberg yelled,

"It was amazing being in the presence of such greats as Spielberg. I had an awesome time."
— Tiwanna Lewis,
East Hartford

"It was cold. But every single minute was worth it."
— Robert Niebrzydowski,
Waterbury

'cut,'" she said. "I just fell, and Tom Cruise reached down and helped me up — he was very, very nice."

Cruise also had some recommendations for Niebrzydowski.

"I asked him what he advice he would have to make it in this business," he said, "and he told me that if you can do anything else in your life, then do it — that this is the toughest business in the world.

"But he also said to follow your heart."

Cruise shouldn't be judged by the recent press he has gotten over his relationship with fiancée Katie Holmes, Niebrzydowski said.

"He is a really nice guy," he said. "He has been getting a lot of funny press lately, but he was really nice to us and took the time to talk to us.

"You really can't listen to everything you hear about him."

Norfolk resident Edie Hofstatter said she still has the hand warmers that Cruise gave out on an especially cold day on the set.

"He and [co-star] Dakota Fanning walked by with big jackets on, and I said to them, 'you look ...'"

"He asked and reach pulled ou warmers.

"I still Tom Cruis

Newspaper Article
War of the Worlds

The landmark for the Uniroyal Factory in Naugatuck,
CT where War of the Worlds was shot

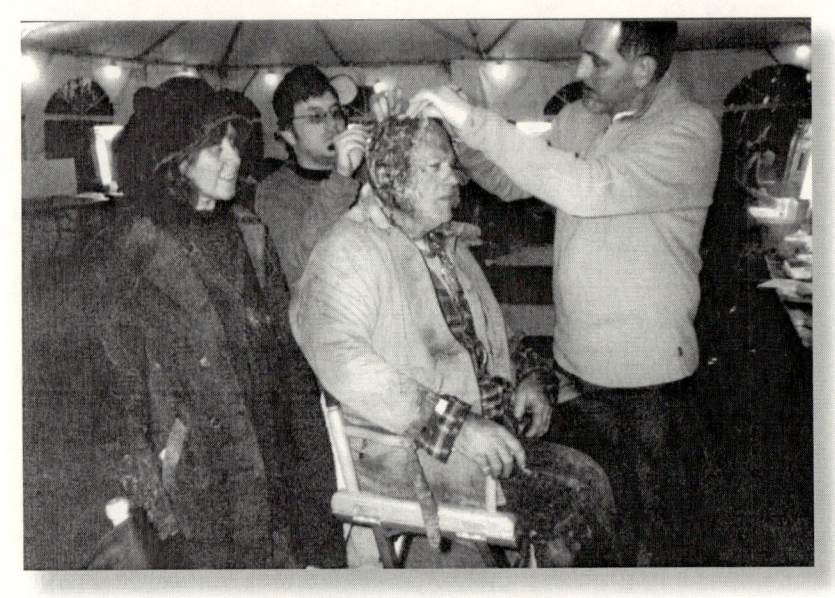

My client, Angelo Ruggiero,
in the make-up chair for War of the Worlds

Stepmom—Limo

One of the movies I had the pleasure of casting for was the movie *Stepmom* with Julia Roberts and Susan Sarandon. It was especially exciting because the New York agency that I was working with had sent a limo bus to pick up the kids at my office in Seymour, Connecticut. No one in the valley had seen limos coming into town to pick up valley kids to act in a major movie. The moms who went as chaperones along with myself were ecstatic. It was like Hollywood! I cast about thirty-five kids for that particular project, and my daughter worked with me on set. I was on the set for the pageant scene with some of the other moms who came on the bus too.

The director, I remember, was very happy with my clients. It felt good to hear how professional they were on set, and the director mentioned this to the crew and myself. Susan and Julia were as beautiful on set as they were on the big screen. The interesting thing about the making of that movie was the way in which Susan and Julia worked with each other. Susan was so brilliant and she was truly a professional who worked so well with the actors who played her children that you could honestly feel the fear that any mother would have with the thoughts that another woman would be taking over her role as a mother. She knew exactly how to come across and played it well.

Julia was as smiling as you would think she would be if you were a fan and followed her in the movies. She often spoke to the cast and had a beautiful, natural quality about her.

Little did I know that during the time of the shoot, that deadly disease was growing in my body—cancer of my uterus. I had some irregular bleeding during the time we were shooting the movie, but I thought it was probably a sign of menopause. I did notice while I was on the set that the bleeding was much more than normal, which frightened me a little.

After the shoot was completed, I called and made an appointment with my doctor to check out what was really going on. He told me he thought it was necessary for me to make an appointment for a procedure called a D&C. The news came to me by phone the next day. The doctor said, "*We have a problem!*" He said I had cancer, and I had to contact an oncology doctor at Yale Hospital. I never thought of the word *oncology*. It was like a foreign language. I was so scared! The world stopped.

Thinking back on it, I realized that I was going through almost the same situation as Susan's character was going through in the movie. Her character had been told that she had cancer and that her chances were not good for survival. My diagnosis was not that severe, but the fear that she depicted in the movie was the same fear I felt. She was trying to cope with the possibility that she would not live long enough to see her son and daughter through college or even marriage. To add to her situation, she was coping with the thoughts of her husband with his new wife, who would be taking over her spot as the mother, which she could not bear.

After party with some of my clients that were on set
for Step Moms

My clients dressed in costume for the Thanksgiving Pageant
scene for Step Moms

One of my child in make-up for <u>Step Moms</u>

The Cancer

Sal and I went to the appointment at Yale together. I was called into the exam room. I was so scared, I couldn't keep my knees from shaking. I sat on the exam table for what seemed an eternity. The doctor finally came into the room. He had my chart in his hand. He asked me a few questions and then asked me to lie down on the exam table. He did a pelvic exam and then told me to get dressed and to come into his office. I went to the waiting room to get Sal. I could see the nervous look on his face.

We sat down in his office, and he started talking to us about the surgery I was going to have because he felt the tumor, and the prior test concluded that I had uterine cancer. He said that there could be some complications after surgery. One complication was that intercourse would be difficult, and it could be also difficult to have an orgasm. He drew a picture of where the tumor was and the place where *he would have to go to remove the tumor, the cervix, and the ovaries, which meant a complete hysterectomy.*

As we sat there, all I could think about was what he said about removing all my female organs and not having the ability to show my love for my husband in a sexual way. Sal and I had always had a beautiful sexual relationship, and what would this mean to us, how it would change our lives. I guess I should have been thinking about my life, but I guess you don't know what your reactions will be when confronted with something so devastating. Yes, I wanted to live, but my life was with the man I loved, and the only thing I could think about was how I could live my life without showing my love.

The surgery was scheduled three weeks after the appointment. It was the worst three weeks of my life. I arrived at the hospital early in the morning and was prepped for surgery. The surgery lasted four hours, when I woke up the doctor came into my room and told me that they got the tumor and the lymph nodes were all clean and that everything looked good. I left the hospital after four days and went home to recover for about four weeks. The sixth week was when I started my radiation therapy to kill any possible lingering cancer cells.

The time came for the radiation treatments. I was told a lot of different stories about the treatment, so I really didn't know what to believe. I was told that it wouldn't be as bad as chemo, but that didn't take away the fear for me. I usually thought of myself as a pretty strong person, but this was a real challenge for me. I arrived at the radiology department in the hospital. The nurse brought me into a dressing room, gave me a gown, and told me to remove my underwear. She brought me into a small room with an exam table in it. She asked me to lie on the table. She then strapped my waist and legs to the table and told me that during the treatment, it was very important not to move because she didn't want the radiation to hit any other organs. She then put a tubelike instrument into my vagina, which I wasn't prepared for; I had no idea this was going to happen. She told me she would be talking to me through a speaker in another adjoining room, and she could see me through a camera. I started to cry when she left the room. I heard the sound of the machine in front of me begin to start the radiation. My body started to shake, and I told the nurse I couldn't stop my knees from shaking. She told me to take deep breaths. Finally, after a couple of minutes, the noise stopped, and I heaved a sigh of relief.

I thought the nurse would come in to take me off the table, but instead, a man dressed in white came into the room with some kind of instrument to measure radiation leakage. He ran the instrument over my body and then spoke into the speaker to tell the nurse I was OK! I asked the nurse what would have happened if there was some leakage. She said, "Well, you would not be allowed to leave the hospital." There were three more treatments to go. I thought, *I made it through this one, I'll make it for the rest. What choice did I have?*

After I was finished with the radiation treatments, my strength started to come back. It was a slow process, but day after day, I began to feel like myself again.

As time went on, Sal and I realized that many of the possible side effects from my surgery did not materialize. I was extremely thankful for that. Sal and I went back to having a loving and fulfilling relationship.

WOMANWISE

WOMANWISE EDITOR
EILEEN FISCHER, 330-6481
efischer@ctpost.com

WEDNESDAY, DECEMBER 3, 2003

Uterine cancer survivor records song of hope for fellow patients

By AMANDA CUDA
acuda@ctpost.com

"Diva" is the last word Liz Tobin-Falzone would ever use to describe herself.

But a battle with uterine cancer and a desire to share her feelings about the disease with as many people as possible led the Beacon Falls resident to step into that role.

Tobin-Falzone, who describes her age as early 50s, wrote and recorded a song earlier this year about her feelings during her struggle with cancer. She says she created the song, "Grateful" (which she also sings), partly because there are few if any pieces of music that deal with these topics.

"We have all these songs, but we never have anything about this disease that takes so many lives," she said.

Since the record was completed, Tobin-Falzone has fought to have as many people hear it as possible, selling it to friends, family and anyone else who seems interested. She's also sent it out to radio stations, television stations, and even wrote a letter to country singer Dolly Parton, asking her opinion (Parton liked it, but said there was little she could do about getting it on the air).

Part of her goal in recording the song is to help those battling cancer to realize that they are not alone.

"When you're going through this, you see all these people around you trying to get close to you, but no one can appreciate what you're going through until they go through it themselves," she said.

Tobin-Falzone was diagnosed with cancer more than four years ago. Throughout the diagnosis and recovery process, she felt an endless stream of emotions — fear that she might not see her family again, gratitude that she had so many people who loved her, and a desire to live each day to the fullest.

Then, nearly a year ago, all of those feelings snowballed together to compel her to write "Grateful."

"One night, inspiration came and I just sprung out of bed," Tobin-Falzone said. "I just started writing straight from my heart."

The lyrics she penned describe the way that cancer can completely alter a life, and the importance of appreciating loved ones, and of showing gratitude to God.

The song is an accurate account of how Tobin-Falzone felt after her diagnosis, she said, and describes how a lot of other cancer patients feel. For instance, she said, the line, "I felt the slam of a brick wall," is an almost universal description of how cancer patients describe their diagnosis.

Christian Abraham/Connecticut Post
Grateful: Liz Tobin-Falzone, of Beacon Falls, has written a song about her experience fighting uterine cancer. She wants other women coping with the

News paper article about the CD I created, called Grateful

Sal and I

The Music

It was about three months after the radiology treatments when one night, I woke up out of a sound sleep and went over to my computer and started to write how I felt about the cancer. The words just kept on coming. I wanted to express my thoughts to other cancer patients and let them know that they were not alone. I wanted to reach out to those loved ones who stood by their family members or friends during the trying times and to tell them the most important thing they can give is their love. A gentle touch of a person who cares because love is the most precious gift of all.

I decided after a few days that I should do something with these feelings. I thought, *If I could bring them to someone else, they could give me some feedback as to what I should do with these thoughts.*

I decided to bring the words to my choir director, who was very understanding and had a very strong faith. She looked over the wording and said, "Liz, why don't you put the words to music?" She told me of a young man who wrote music and gave me his number.

I contacted a young man named Sal Grillo, and we decided to meet and discuss the possibilities. We went to his house where he had his piano, and he looked over the wording and said to me, "We could put this to music." We started meeting once a week, and finally, the music to the words came together beautifully. I found out during our time together that Sal's family had been touched by cancer also.

It now was time for a studio to record the CD. We hired a drummer to play for us, and finally, it all came together, and I entitled the song "Grateful."

Auditions for a female vocalist were held. The auditions went pretty well, but somehow, we thought the feelings just didn't come through from the vocalist we auditioned.

The head of the studio said, "Liz, you sing professionally, it would be great if you sing the song. It is your creation."

I decided that the ending of the song needed something special. Some of my clients had family members that were either diagnosed with cancer or had family members who were touched by cancer. I contacted the clients and asked if they would be interested in doing the background lyrics of the song. Only a few had professional training, but all together, it sounded great, and most of all, it sounded real.

I needed a cover for the CD. I had a friend in town, Dominick Sorrentino, who I had worked with through Park and Recreation on various volunteer projects. He was very artistic and was a graphic designer.

We got together, and I explained to him what the song was meant to express. He took the wording of the song and created a meaningful and expressive cover using a baby, stars, birds, flowers, and the holding of hands as an expression of love. The cover was then complete. It turned out to be absolutely beautiful.

The CD took off. I sold the CD, and partial profits went toward various cancer organizations.

The CD got a lot of attention. The story about the birth of the CD was featured on Channel 8 News.

The doctor and nurses at Yale, where my surgery took place, loved it, and the doctor referred me to the publicity department in Yale to do a story.

I made my singing appearance in my hometown on family day, and it got rave reviews.

I also was called by the television daytime show called Connecticut Style, and I performed the song live in the studio.

People sometimes stop me on the street and ask if they could have a copy for their friend or family member. I would, many times, give the CD for free.

The CD didn't make much money, but it didn't matter to me because whoever it had helped in some small way was what it was meant to do.

GRATEFUL

My Darling, My Love,
The day I answered the phone,
The day our lives were forever torn.
I felt the sting of a brick wall.
I was sure nothing else mattered
ever matter at all.

But I should have known,
that God leaves no one alone.
I am so grateful to have him in my life
He's healed my soul, he's been there
through it all. He's given new
meaning to my life

(Long Chorus)
Baby if I could say what's in my heart,
I would say to love what you've got.
I would tell everyone young and old,
Know the life Gods made for you,
The ones above that sing for you.
The birds above who sing for you,
And most of all enjoy the touch of
the ones who love you

The cancer that destroyed our happiness
and ripped like a knife through our lives
Could not destroy the love in your eyes
you had your tears, but I left your fears,
So remember my love, that God leaves
no one alone. I am so grateful to have
you in my life. When I look at your
smiling face and look into your eyes.
My heart grows wings and flies.

(Repeat Long Chorus)

For life is precious, love is sweet,
Love is the only thing that evil or
man can't defeat.

So baby if I could say what's in my heart,
I would say to love what you've got.
And most of all enjoy that touch of
the ones who love you.
And most of all enjoy the touch of
the ones who love you

(Repeat Long Chorus)

LIZ FALZONE

Composer's song an attempt to touch people's hearts

Continued from C1

"Most people hit with what could be a terminal situation do use that phrase," she said.

When she finished the lyrics, Tobin-Falzone wanted to set them to music, but couldn't write music. A friend suggested she contact Sal Grillo of West Haven, who writes and teaches music. When Tobin-Falzone brought the song to Grillo, he agreed to do it almost immediately.

Grillo said his reasons for taking on the project were mostly personal. His mother had recently died from cancer and his mother-in-law is currently battling the disease.

Working on the song was his attempt to provide understanding and comfort to those suffering from cancer.

"I don't know what it's like," Grillo said. "But I think there's people who listen to this and say 'This is what I'm going through.'"

A talent manager who does casting for movies, commercials and other projects, Tobin-Falzone also used to sing professionally.

Originally, she hadn't planned to sing on "Grateful," but she was recruited after none of the singers auditioned worked out. She and Grillo chose four women — including Grillo's stepdaughter, Tara Piscatelli, 13 — to sing backup.

Most of the backup singers have some connection to cancer — either having battled it themselves, or knowing someone who has the disease.

Piscatelli has a grandmother fighting lung and brain cancer. She said she likes what the song has to say about cancer and about life.

"It's just about living every day meaningfully and making it count," Piscatelli said.

Tobin-Falzone is working hard to get her song heard. She said that many of those who have heard it so far have found it moving, particularly those who have been touched by cancer. So far, that has been the most gratifying part of releasing the song.

"That's what I wanted to do — touch people's hearts," Tobin-Falzone said.

Making a difference

Tom Kabelka / Republican-American

Griffin Hospital's Women Making a Difference in the Valley held a luncheon Thursday at the Grass Hill Lodge in Derby to honor seven women. Seated, from the left, are: Jean Banks of Seymour for her work with Girl Scouts, Connecticut Trails Council; Mary Deming, longtime teacher in the Seymour High School Science Department; and Suzanne Reilly, a Seymour resident who has done extensive work in the Valley Y Community. Back row: Kathy Veriezza, a teacher in the Business Department at Seymour High School; Sue Mis, town nurse at the senior center in Beacon Falls; Liz Tobin-Falzone, active in Beacon Falls volunteer work, including efforts to reach out to less fortunate families and work with Family Services and health professionals for homebound patients; Naomi Wallace of Ansonia, arts director at the Tinney Center for encouraging children to discover their talents, and who served eight years on the Valley Chapter of the American Red Cross.

God, Please Not Again

Sal and I usually did, and still do, mostly everything together. We were due for our yearly physical. We went to the appointment thinking that everything would be all right. It was about three days after the visit, and the phone call came in from the doctor. I knew that something had to be wrong. The doctor recommended a specialist. He said that Sal had a high PSA reading from his blood work and thought it would be a good idea to have a biopsy of his prostate.

The first visit with the specialist was scary for Sal. He was examined by the doctor, and the doctor agreed that a biopsy was needed.

I was so scared for Sal; I didn't want him to go through all the pain and fear that this disease can cause.

Well, my fears came true. Sal had cancer. He had 87 percent cancer located on the left side of the prostate and would need surgery. The doctor recommended a surgical procedure called the da Vinci Surgery, which was performed by a type of robot. He said that this procedure would be less invasive, and the recovery time would be a lot shorter. Dr. Arthur Pinto recommended that Sal and I attended an informative workshop on the technology behind the da Vinci robot surgery. He informed us that there was a workshop regarding the da Vinci robot surgery that was being held in a couple of weeks in a nearby hotel. So I made reservations for Sal and me to attend.

At the workshop we were given the opportunity to operate the robot. The hand of the robot could actually make a three hundred and sixty degree turn, which would help the surgeon operating the robot to reach areas that could be difficult to reach otherwise. The video of the actual surgery showed the cancerous prostate being put in a bag so to retrieve any cancer cells.

Sal and I talked over all the options and decided that the da Vinci was the right procedure for him.

The day came for the operation, and we arrived at the hospital early in the morning. Sal was taken into surgery, and I went down to the chapel to pray. Tears were streaming down my face. I prayed like I had never prayed before. I just wanted to see this man whom I loved so much to come out of the surgery and be free of this threatening disease.

I went back up to the waiting room and sat there with our daughter for what seemed like an eternity. The doctor finally came into the room. All I could see was his eyes. He said that the surgery went well, and they removed any possible lingering cancer cells.

I started to cry again, but with joy this time that this man I loved would be by my side again, healthy and smiling and looking forward to all the beautiful things that life had in store for us.

After Sal's recovery, the doctor who performed the surgery asked if he would be interested in talking to some of his other patients who were going to have the same robot surgery for prostate cancer that he did. He was happy to answer some of those important questions that many male patients are concerned about. He wanted to alleviate the fear of the surgery and the recovery. He still, to this day, gets calls from men, young and old, who are faced with this disease.

A Little Bit of Heaven

Sal and I were looking for a new place to call home. We finally found a little town called Beacon Falls. The town was hardly noticeable as you would pass through on Route 8. It was a beautiful place nestled in the beautiful Naugatuck Valley.

We found a house we really loved, a little white colonial that had a beautiful backyard surrounded by trees and a little stream in the back of the property.

One day, as we were driving home, we saw a young man walking his pet cow up from downtown Main Street. We loved it! My daughter, Sal, and I couldn't take our eyes off the young man and his pet cow. I knew then and there we had chosen the right place to call home.

Sal and I got involved with the town right away. I volunteered for St. Michael's Church choir, Park and Recreation, Inland Wetland, Lioness Club, was nominated for church counsel, chairperson for Citizens for Tomorrow's Downtown, and was a member of St. Michael's Church Ladies Guild and Sal and I were given an honorable membership to the Beacon Falls Senior Center.

I was even given the honor of an official citation in recognition of making a difference in the valley and having demonstrated significant achievements in my field of endeavors signed by the secretary of state.

I even managed to finish my college degree in business administration.

It wasn't long before I had the privilege of knowing almost everyone in town. Christmas was especially fun. The firehouse did, and still does to this day, a Christmas parade. Everyone walks to town hall and the two churches in town, St. Michael's and the Beacon Falls Congregational Church, for the lighting of Christmas trees and the singing of carols. The firehouse would then have lots of hot chocolate and doughnuts ready for all.

Sal would volunteer to wear costumes for almost any occasion. He was the duck for the annual duck race. He was, as I called him, an Italian leprechaun. He even was a geisha girl for one of the many skits I directed for the Lions' annual convention in which, by the way, we always won first prize for best skit.

My daughter made friends easily and, to this day, remains friends with many of the kids she once went to high school with.

The town had been a place of healing for us. It has seen us through good and trying times. It is a peaceful and joyful place where nature surrounds us with a beautiful array of birds, deer, rabbits, and other bits of God's creation.

I have heard people say that living in such a small community is difficult because everyone knows each other's business. I personally think it's great because even if one knows your business, in times of trouble, they are there to help in any way they can.

So as I sit in my dining room with my cathedral windows looking out into the forest at the trees decorated with clouds of white snow and my Christmas tree decorated with all the loving memories of my life with Sal and Shauna, I feel a sense of peace and abundance of love and thankfulness for all those things I never thought were possible to even possess.

I now have a beautiful grandson, John Thomas, and my daughter is a loving and caring mother. I am so proud of the woman she has become. I know that good and beautiful things will happen to her and her family in the future years to come.

I have always told her to have faith, always dance when you have the chance, and love life every waking day because life, dreams, and hope is the food for the soul, so let it soar!

The kid from the poor class neighborhood with the abusive and alcoholic parents made a difference, maybe in a small or big way; I guess I will never really know, but I am thankful for all those silent cries and those tears from all the angels that surround me day by day.

So what does it mean? Silent cries are heard. It doesn't matter what god you believe in; he is there, reminding us that for every tear we drop, there is hope for another day. After all, isn't it about how we earn our steps to heaven one step at a time?

Some members of the St. Michael's Church Choir in Beacon Falls
Debbie, Kathy and Liz

St. Michael's Church in beacon Falls Anniversity Dinner.
We performed skits related to the nineteen-forties in connection
to the church's Anniversity Harrold, Eddie, Gary, Maureen,
Nancy, Maria Top Row Bob, Sal and Liz

Rubber duckies lead way to fun at annual festival in Beacon Falls

By Jean Falbo-Sosnovich
Register Correspondent

BEACON FALLS — Blue skies and warm sunshine helped things go swimmingly Saturday for the town's fourth annual duck race and downtown festival.

More than 1,500 rubber ducks, complete with black wrap-around sunglasses, filled the bill for the event, staged by the Beacon Falls Lions Club and Citizens for Tomorrow's Downtown committee.

The event is held each year to raise funds to revitalize downtown.

The day's festivities kicked off early with a townwide tag sale, and by noon, hundreds of spectators began crowding behind the senior center and firehouse to browse at up to 30 craft and food booths, while listening to the jazzy sounds of Danbury's own, the Bearcats.

A giant dragon moon bounce, courtesy of the Beacon Falls Lioness Club, and face painting by the Beacon Falls Library staff, kept children entertained, as did the noisy duck whistles for sale. Donald Duck was also on hand, quacking youngsters up and posing for photos.

The main event — the duck race — was under way just after 3 p.m. Members of the Lions Club braved the chilly waters of the Naugatuck River to dump crates of ducks into a large cage, decked out in American flags, sitting in the middle of the river.

More than 500 spectators, who lined the riverbank, did a countdown and the ducks were launched. The swift-moving water moved the ducks along quickly to their destination just past the Depot Street bridge. Children raced along the river to get a glimpse of the fast ducks, which melded into one big sea of yellow.

Prizes, including a complete Dell computer system, an antique roll-top desk, and Broadway tickets to "'The Lion King," were awarded to the owners of the lucky ducks that placed in first through sixth place. People purchased duck adoption certificates throughout the festival, as well as at downtown businesses prior to the event.

Alexandra Szabo, 6, along with her grandmother, Sue Hoinsky, enjoyed taking in the sights and sounds.

"'The moon bounce is so fun," Alexandra said, while Hoinsky, a newcomer to Beacon Falls, said the event is "a wonderful thing for the community."

Resident Sheryl Feducia was on hand with her daughter, Lindsay, 9, and Lindsay's friend, Sam Muggio, 10. Sam's duck came in fourth place last year, and she won a Sony Playstation 2, but she wasn't as lucky this year.

"I come for the snacks," Sam said, munching on some cookies.

Downtown Committee Chairman and Lion Rick Cherhoniak was pleased with the turnout.

"We had a beautiful day, the weather was great, sales were good and the event brought a lot of people downtown," Cherhoniak said.

The festival was started four years ago to raise awareness about plans to renovate downtown, which has already included creation of Volunteer Park and spruced up medians and new landscaping.

Jean Falbo-Sosnovich can be reached at jean.sos@snet.net.

BEACON FALLS—*Blue skies and warm sunshine helped things go swimmingly Saturday for the town's fourth annual duck race and downtown festival.*

More than 1,500 rubber ducks, complete with black wrap-around sunglasses, filled the bill for the event, staged by the Beacon Falls Lions Club and Citizens for Tomorrow's Downtown committee.

The event is held each year to raise funds to revitalize downtown.

The day's festivities kicked off early with a townwide tag sale, and by noon, hundreds of spectators began crowding behind the senior center and firehouse to browse at up to 30 craft and food booths, while listening to the jazzy sounds of Danbury's own, the Bearcats.

A giant dragon moon bounce, courtesy of the Beacon Falls Lioness Club, and face painting by the Beacon Falls Library staff, kept children entertained, as did the noisy duck whistles for sale. Donald Duck was also on hand, quacking youngsters up and posing for photos.

The main event—the duck race—was under way just after 3 p.m. Members of the Lions Club braved the chilly waters of the Naugatuck River to dump crates of ducks into a large cage, decked out in American flags, sitting in the middle of the river.

More than 500 spectators, who lined the riverbank, did a countdown and the ducks were launched. The swift-moving water moved the ducks along quickly to their destination just past the Depot Street bridge. Children raced along the river to get a glimpse of the fast ducks, which melded into one big sea of yellow.

Prizes, including a complete Dell computer system, an antique roll-top desk, and Broadway tickets to "The Lion King," were awarded to the owners of the lucky ducks that placed in first through sixth place. People purchased duck adoption certificates throughout the festival, as well as at downtown businesses prior to the event.

Alexandra Szabo, 6, along with her grandmother, Sue Hoinsky, enjoyed taking in the sights and sounds.

"The moon bounce is so fun," Alexandra said, while Hoinsky, a newcomer to Beacon Falls, said the event is "a wonderful thing for the community."

Resident Sheryl Feducia was on hand with her daughter, Lindsay, 9, and Lindsay's friend, Sam Muggio, 10. Sam's duck came in fourth place last year, and she won a Sony Playstation 2, but she wasn't as lucky this year.

"I come for the snacks," Sam said, munching on some cookies.

Downtown Committee Chairman and Lion Rick Cherhoniak was pleased with the turnout.

"We had a beautiful day, the weather was great, sales were good and the event brought a lot of people downtown," Cherhoniak said.

The festival was started four years ago to raise awareness about plans to renovate downtown, which has already included creation of Volunteer Park and spruced up medians and new landscaping.

Lioness at the Beacon Falls Firemen's Parade
1. Sue (Top) 2. Elaine (Bottom) 3. Gayle (bottom) 4. Millie 5. Liz

Lioness Club
1. Martha 2. Liz 3. Elaine 4. Debbie

Lions Convention doing a skit from Grease.
We won first prize! Which I Directed

Lions Convention
Viva Las Vegas dance routine
1. Kathleen 2. Sue
That I directed and won first price

My dear Friends Jo and Jack who always made me laugh
who have always been there to lend a helping hand
and to support my endeavors. (in costume)

New Pals

Paul Bedryczuk and his son, Zachary, two, visited with Donald Duck at the fourth annual duck race in Beacon Falls, Saturday.

Sal dressed as the duck for the annual duck race in Beacon Falls.

Flowers to Roar About

Joe Poirier, left, and Sal Falzone of the Beacon Falls Lions Club set up flowers for their annual Easter Sale. The stand, located adjacent to the Main Street Fire House in Beacon Falls, will be open Friday and Saturday from 9:00 a.m. to 6:00 p.m. The flowers will be from $3 to $10.

Sal selling flowers for the Lions of Beacon Falls, Connecticut.

Forgiveness Why Not!

My mother throughout her later years became ill with heart disease, a broken hip, and partial blindness in one eye. She needed care, and as you can guess, I was the only one who could take care of her. I could have turned my back and said no, but I was very aware that everyone has to answer to a much higher authority for their actions. It wasn't up to me to pass judgment. My mother unknowingly had made me a stronger and more loving and giving person.

My daughter luckily got to see her grandmother in a more vulnerable state, and I am happy to say that their relationship was wonderful. My daughter loved her grandma, and my mom showed love and tenderness to her. I had never spoken badly about her grandmother in her early childhood years. When my mother passed on, my daughter had only good memories, and I thanked God for that. I won't ever forget, but forgiveness is what I have achieved.

Biography

Liz is of Irish descent, born here in the United States. Liz is an actress and a professional singer.

She is a survivor of uterine cancer and has made a musical CD in recognition of all cancer survivors entitled "Grateful."

Liz maintains her religious beliefs in her daily life and has an abundance of love for people and nature, being true to her astrological sign Taurus.

She has received numerous awards, such as Connecticut Area Director for Talent Reviews and acknowledgment letters from her peers in the business, who have made note of her caring and professional treatment of her clients.

She also has received first place awards for her direction in various productions. Liz has also been awarded by the State of Connecticut General Assembly for her contributions, professional and volunteer, for making a significant difference, and achievements in her community. She has been an active member of several local organizations as well as having served as the president of the Lioness Club in Beacon Falls.

Liz is a loving mother and wife, who has successfully combined her family life with her business life and has been nominated Mother of the Year for a prominent magazine. She has also successfully helped her daughter in obtaining her college degree in biology and the pursuit of her professional endeavors.

Edwards Brothers Malloy
Thorofare, NJ USA
December 13, 2012